THE GOTHAM LIBRARY
OF THE NEW YORK UNIVERSITY PRESS

The Gotham Library is a series of original works and critical studies published in paperback primarily for student use. The Gotham hardcover edition is primarily for use by libraries and the general reader. Devoted to significant works and major authors and to literary topics of enduring importance, Gotham Library texts offer the best in literature and criticism.

Comparative and Foreign Language Literature:
  Robert J. Clements, Editor

Comparative and English Language Literature:
  James W. Tuttleton, Editor

War in
Melville's Imagination

Joyce Sparer Adler

New York University Press · New York *and* London

Copyright © 1981 by New York University
Library of Congress Cataloging in Publication Data
Adler, Joyce Sparer
  War in Melville's Imagination.

  (The Gotham library of the New York University
Press)
  Includes bibliographical references and index.
  1. Melville, Herman, 1819-1891—Criticism and
interpretation. 2. War in literature. I. Title.
PS2388.W37A34   813′.3   80-20656
ISBN 0-8147-0574-X
ISBN 0-8147-0575-8 (pbk.)
Manufactured in the United States of America

To Ellen
who was like a forerunner
of what human beings may someday be

Acknowledgments

My immeasurable professional debt is to Merton M. Sealts who, ever since I first informed him of my undertaking, has made me the most generous, repeated, purely voluntary gifts of time and invaluable advice and who spurred me on at difficult times. I am happy to have had the warm encouragement and shared ideas of Carolyn Karcher, Donald Yannella, Hennig Cohen, Howard P. Vincent, Sidney Kaplan, Liane Norman, and Bruce Franklin. The late Luther S. Mansfield was very helpful to me. The novelist-poet Wilson Harris opened my eyes to many of the workings of the poetic imagination. I thank my husband, Irving Adler, for personal help day after day and for his intellectual share in this book. I was lucky to have Eleanor Moore to type and retype the manuscript. And I deeply appreciate the younger members of my family who, so patiently, continued to be interested and cooperative: Laura, Naomi, David, Martin, and Nbalia.

The last chapter of this book first appeared in *PMLA*, March 1976 as "*Billy Budd* and Melville's Philosophy of War" (Copyright © 1975 by the Modern Language Association of America). An earlier version of Chapter 1 appeared in *The Minnesota Review*, as "Melville's *Typee* and *Omoo*: Of 'Civilized' War on 'Savage' Peace" (Copyright 1978). Earlier versions of Chapters 6 and 7 appeared in *Science and Society* as "Melville on the White Man's War against the American Indian" and "*Benito Cereno*: Slavery and Violence in the Americas" (Copyright 1971 and 1974). Chapter 8 is a full development of a theme first set forth in the first part of my article in *New Letters* "Melville and the Civil War" (Copyright 1973). I wish to thank the editors and staff of these journals, and also and especially Despina Papazoglou of New York University Press, for their warmth, interest, and help.

. . . the visible world of experience being that procreative thing which impregnates the muses.

—Herman Melville, Pierre, XVIII, Section I

Contents

Prelude

The War-or-Peace Theme in Melville

War or peace? This question—primal in the relationship between man and man in Melville's vision of the world of his age—
runs like a transcontinental river through his work. In many places
it flows in the open; these have been explored and the findings
variously, often oppositely, interpreted. Since, however, much of its
course is not in the open but shrouded as if by mist or jungle, its
existence as a continuous current of extraordinary depth, force,
and influence on what surrounds it has not been perceived. But
"still it moves"; sooner or later someone had to be carried down it,
even if only by accident, as Orellana was led to travel the Amazon
from Quito to the Atlantic.

This book traces my exploration of the war-or-peace theme in
Melville's work from the time it springs up in the second chapter of
Typee, in the picture of the warships in the harbor of Nukuheva,
"out of keeping" with the beauty of the island, to the time it goes
fathoms down in the sea at the end of *Billy Budd,* in the picture of
the young sailor enchained in the oozy weeds, symbol of how "out
of keeping" (the early phrase reappears in *Billy Budd)* beauty and
good necessarily are in a world dedicated to "that which prac-
tically is the abrogation of everything but brute Force."

1

The sustained, underlying theme of *Typee/Omoo* is the contrast between the wars of conquest and occupation of the South Seas by "white, civilized man" and the tropical peace the nineteenth-century imperialists destroyed. "War or peace" is the question that unifies *Mardi* and reveals its hidden design, the center around which the particles in *White-Jacket* revolve, the challenge to man's imagination expressed in *Moby-Dick,* world literature's symbolic poem of war and peace. *Israel Potter* obliquely asks: What gain was there for the common soldiers and sailors "exiled" from the benefits won by the American Revolution? *Benito Cereno* makes visible the inseparability of violence and slavery in the Americas, and, by suggestion, of violence and enslavement in the world. The Swiftian grotesque art of the "Indian-hating" section in the context of *The Confidence-Man* implies how grotesquely the "history" of the war of extermination waged against the original Americans has been and continues to be told, and for what grim purpose, as well as to what ill effect on the United States. *Battle-Pieces,* in the form of tragic drama, enacts the "enlightening" agony of the Civil War from the original sin of slavery to the hope of "promoted life." Finally the poetry of *Billy Budd* as a whole (narrative and ballad together) intimates the possibility that the question of what war means to humanity may begin to stir in the consciousness of the crew of man and eventually find utterance.

In some ways the war-or-peace theme in Melville's art is changeless, in some ways ever changing. His need to probe the meaning and structures of the world of his day and its relation to the universe and Time is continuous. Abhorrence of war; belief that as long as brute Force remains dominant in the world, enslavement of human by human will continue; questionings about whether man's voice will ever be raised effectively against war—all these flow from beginning to end. Also carried from work to work are patterns of conceptual images associated in Melville's imagination with war and peace. But the distribution of light and shadow varies in the continuum, in proportion to the admixture of hope and despair Melville felt at a particular period; in each work the war-or-peace theme has a unique artistic expression; and although countless poetic concepts are borne into the last work from almost every earlier one, Melville's philosophy of war in *Billy Budd* is qualitatively different from what it ever was before.

Melville's passion against war was a great dynamic in his imagination and a main shaping force in his art.

1.

Typee and *Omoo:* Of "Civilized" War on "Savage" Peace

Towards noon we drew abreast the entrance to the harbor, and at last we slowly swept by the intervening promontory, and entered the bay of Nukuheva. No description can do justice to its beauty; but that beauty was lost to me then, and I saw nothing but the tri-colored flag of France trailing over the stern of six vessels, whose black hulls and bristling broadsides proclaimed their warlike character. There they were, floating in that lovely bay, the green eminences of the shore looking down so tranquilly upon them, as if rebuking the sternness of their aspect. *To my eye nothing could be more out of keeping than the presence of these vessels;* but we soon learnt what brought them there. The whole group of islands had just been taken possession of by Rear-Admiral Du Petit Thouars, in the name of the invincible French nation. *(Typee,* ii, 12) [1]

The war-or-peace theme in Melville's work that makes its first appearance in the passage quoted becomes the underlying theme of *Typee* (1846) and *Omoo* (1847). In them the opposition and choice take this more concrete form: "civilized" wars of colonialist domination or the fulfillment of the inherent human desire for peaceful relations among men, as evidenced in the daily life of "savage" groups not yet corrupted by modern civilization. Beneath the adventure story in *Typee* and its sequel, beneath the geographical and anthropological descriptions—often, even, beneath the humor—is Melville's interpretation of what occurred in the South Pacific from the early 1800s to the time when he, a twenty-three-year-old sailor, glimpsed warships in the midst of tropical beauty and tranquillity. The early spectacle influenced his perspective on all he would see in Polynesia and became an essential part of his vision of the nineteenth-century world. It brought to consciousness what would be the feeling of a lifetime, that nothing could be more out of keeping with good and beauty than what the warships signified; war, as the footnote to *Omoo*'s Chapter xxix defines it, is the "greatest of evils." [2] The picture of the frigates in the harbor of Nukuheva, if well executed by a graphic artist, could serve as a frontispiece for Melville's first two books printed as one.

Together, *Typee* and *Omoo* present the three stages of Polynesian history as Melville interpreted them, all of which he could observe side by side as he moved from island to island and from shore to interior. The first is life in a "state of nature," as in the everyday life of the people of the remote Typee valley. The second is the stage of widening encroachment by "civilization," whose purpose it is to exploit the islands and the islanders. The third is the period of complete occupation rule, resulting in the dying out of Polynesians, so fully and movingly described in *Omoo*. Each work reverberates the other's special theme, and both merge into the one they share. *Typee* predicts the extermination of the Typees because of what civilization soon will bring; *Omoo* looks back on the peace and happiness the Tahitians enjoyed before the coming of the white Christian invaders. Both books show civilization and Christianity in the South Seas as the opposite, in effect, of what they pretend to be. Civilization, presumably the ameliorator of life, brings death; Christianity, presumably the bearer of light, puts out the sun—the culture—which the Polynesians need in order to live. Melville's history of the war the nineteenth-century colonialists waged on the people of the South Pacific is the real, though not the external story of *Typee/Omoo*. Its implications, however, are not for that area of the world alone.

The implied theme of *Typee* is: Who are the real cannibals, the Typees who practice a ritual of eating the flesh of their dead attackers or the aggressor nations who have come to devour the islands? The answer, offered implicitly by the book as a whole, is also offered explicitly: "The fiend-like skill we display in the invention of all manner of death-dealing engines, the vindictiveness with which we carry on our wars, and the misery and desolation that follow in their train, are enough of themselves to distinguish the white civilized man as the most ferocious animal on the face of the earth" (xvii, 125).

Typee's subtitle, *A Peep at Polynesian Life,* half shows, half hides, Melville's intention. The bulk of the work—twenty-two out of thirty-four chapters—concerns the life of the Typees, in which absence of class distinctions or rigid family divisions, the practice of cooperation, and equal sharing of food and land typify the general spirit and organization of life. But Melville is no primitivist: modern civilization is from first to last, in all his work, his main concern. His account of the Typees' customs, crafts, traditions, pleasures, and rituals is the basis for a comparative study: the peaceful day-to-day life of the Typees is a vantage point from which to see more clearly the destructive aspects of nineteenth-century Christian civilization. *Typee* could just as easily be subtitled *A Peep at Civilization by Means of a Peep at Polynesian Life.*

At the beginning of *Typee* it appears that France alone is to be the target of Melville's condemnation of the war in the South Seas. He recounts her takeover of the Marquesas, unmasking her pretenses at humanity, Christianity, refinement, fairness, truth, and valor. Her occupation of the islands is "iniquitous" and "a signal infraction of the rights of humanity." He tells how she set up a puppet ruler and then sent warships to defend him; he anticipates other subterfuges the French will commit "to defend whatever cruelties they may hereafter think fit to commit in bringing the Marquesan natives into subjection"; and he explains that it was under cover of a similar pretense that the French "perpetrated" their "outrages and massacres at Tahiti the beautiful" (iii, 17–18). The Nukuhevans detest those who have made this "cavalier appropriation" of their shores and want to defend their land, but they are helpless in the face of the military might of the French. Thus, early in *Typee,* Melville begins to develop his idea that brute Force alone makes possible human enslavement and its accompanying ills: in his vision of the world, war is not only the greatest of evils; it is the original one.

But it becomes apparent that France, whose annexation of the Marquesas Melville happened to witness, is representative of all the nations that have come to "prey like bears," as *Mardi* will soon say. Other than French atrocities are narrated, the first and most outstanding among them being those committed by Capt. David Porter and his men from the U.S. frigate *Essex* who some years earlier attempted unsuccessfully to subjugate the Typees. Forced to retreat and abandon their "design of conquest," these "invaders, on their march back to the sea, consoled themselves for their repulse by setting fire to every house and temple in their route; and a long line of smoking ruins defaced . . . the valley, and proclaimed to its pagan inhabitants the spirit that reigned in the breasts of Christian soldiers." Melville generalizes:

> How often is the term "savages" incorrectly applied! None really deserving of it were ever yet discovered by voyagers or by travellers. They have discovered heathens and barbarians, whom by horrible cruelties they have exasperated into savages. It may be asserted without fear of contradiction, that in all the cases of outrages committed by Polynesians, Europeans have at some time or other been the aggressors, and that the cruel and bloodthirsty disposition of some of the islanders is mainly to be ascribed to the influence of such examples. (iv, 27)

The Typees in their remote valley have not yet been influenced by these examples. Melville wonders at their humaneness, and a conception that will at his most despairing be absent from his work but that will achieve great imaginative expression in *Moby-Dick* and *Billy Budd* appears in expository form in *Typee.* He voices his belief in humanity's latent original virtue in response to the question of how to explain the enigma that among the heathen Typees all went on with a harmony "unparalleled . . . in the most select, refined, and pious associations of mortals in Christendom." It must have been the result of an "inherent principle of honesty and charity" that is "graven on every breast" but that can be "distorted by arbitrary codes." It is to this "indwelling, this universally diffused perception of what is *just* and *noble,* that the integrity of the Marquesans in their intercourse with each other is to be attributed" (xxvii, 200–201).

The Typees are fortunate that they have not yet had the religion proclaimed by the imperialist nations forced upon them, for the imposition of Christianity upon "pagan" peoples is a death-dealing process as Melville describes it (xxvi, 195–96). The Anglo-Saxons "have extirpated Paganism from the greater part of the North American continent; but with it they have likewise extirpated the greater portion of the Red race." Similarly, the result of attempts that were presumably to "ameliorate the spiritual condition of the Polynesians . . . has almost invariably been to accomplish their temporal destruction!" The islander who still lives "finds himself an interloper in the country of his fathers." The fruits of the earth where he was born are "remorselessly seized upon and appropriated by the stranger, are devoured before the eyes of the starving inhabitants, or sent on board the numerous vessels which now touch at their shores." The Polynesian is told to work for next to nothing; the only alternative he has is to starve. "Not until I visited Honolulu was I aware of the fact that the small remnant of the natives had been civilized into draught horses, and evangelized into beasts of burden." The destruction of peoples has become worldwide: "Civilization is gradually sweeping from the earth the lingering vestiges of Paganism, and at the same time the shrinking forms of its unhappy worshippers." Melville is troubled to think of the dread fate the Typees face when in a few years Christian civilization inevitably "shall have driven all peace and happiness from the valley."

This fate, as illustrated in Tahiti and confirmed in Hawaii and other Polynesian islands, is the main subject of *Omoo,* which, grasped as a whole, is nothing less than a charge of genocide. Melville calls the process "depopulation" and attributes it to the starvation brought by civilization; to the corruption and demoralization caused by the invaders; and to the destruction of Polynesian culture, a process he terms *denationalization.*

Melville's "Preface" to *Omoo* shows his main purpose to be social enlightenment, not entertainment: "As a roving sailor, the author spent about three months in various parts of the islands of Tahiti and Imeeo . . . under circumstances most favorable for correct observations on the social condition of the natives" (p. xiv).[3] His letter submitting *Omoo* to John Murray, his British publisher, indicates that he intended the theme of the book to be Polynesian life "as affected by intercourse with the whites" ("Historical Note," p. 330).

In Tahiti, as in the Marquesas, the aggressor nation in 1842 is France. But once again that country is not Melville's sole target. The cession of Tahiti to the French, just concluded when the narrator arrives, is acceded to by Britain, for "mighty interests" of her own, despite her repeated past assurances to the island that she would guarantee its independence (xxxii, 124). The United States, too, plays a war-promoting role: the French warship, the *Reine Blanche*, is "one of the heavy sixty-gun frigates now in vogue all over the world . . . which we Yankees were the first to introduce. In action, these are the most murderous vessels ever lanched" (xxix, 109). The genocidal effects of economic and cultural domination are well advanced by the time the French arrive. The "most distressing consequence of civilization" in places like Tahiti—lack of food, previously unknown—is now "ever present," because "the demands of the shipping exhaust the uncultivated resources of the island" (xxxiv, 131–32). Christian missionaries have been the allies of the exploiters. There have been religious wars. In a valley of the island of Imeeo, Melville sees that rich with trees as it is, few are useful to the natives, and he wonders why none is a coconut or breadfruit tree. The scene from the past, described to him as the answer, symbolizes the intentional destruction of life brought about by Christian crusaders from Tahiti: "In the sanguinary religious hostilities which ensued upon the conversion to Christianity of the first Pomaree, a war party from Tahiti destroyed (by 'girdling' the bark) entire groves of these invaluable trees. For some time afterward, they stood stark and leafless in the sun; sad monuments of the fate which befell the inhabitants of the valley" (lv, 214).

Deprived of an adequate supply of food, the Tahitians have

been wasting away. But what Melville stresses especially is that the attacks on their culture, the "denationalizing" process (xlvii, 183) supervised by the missionaries and enforced by the religious police, has destroyed the Polynesians' will to live. Innocent sports and pastimes—wrestling, foot racing, throwing the javelin, archery, dancing, tossing the football, kite flying, flute playing, and singing traditional songs—have been made punishable offenses. Necklaces and garlands of flowers, tattooing, and national costumes, modest enough to Melville, are forbidden. The breadfruit harvest festival has been suppressed. Old beliefs, arts, and traditions are made to seem evil or valueless. Privacy is invaded by the religious constabulary. Personal names disapproved of by the missionaries are changed to biblical names meaningless to those renamed and hence ridiculous to Melville (lxxiii, 277). The abolition of their culture has not been "willingly acquiesced in" by the Tahitians (xlvii, 183). Conformity has been achieved by terror. Melville relates how under Pomaree II "by force of arms, was Christianity finally triumphant"; there was "great slaughter" in these "religious wars" (lxxx, 302).

Demoralized, idle, or indulging in sensualities not known to them before the advent of the white man, the Polynesians, it seems to Melville, cannot long exist (xlix, 190–92). According to Captain Cook, in 1777 the population of Tahiti was about two hundred thousand; "By a regular census taken some four or five years ago, it was found to be only nine thousand." The evils causing the Tahitians' extinction are "solely of foreign origin," as is the venereal disease "which now taints the blood of at least two thirds of the common people of the island." In the context of race extinction in which Melville describes the sufferings brought by it in *Omoo*, the "poison" of syphilis comes close to being a symbol of all the corrupting and death-bringing influences of "intercourse with the whites"; indeed, what the composite canvas of *Typee* and *Omoo* depicts is the rape of Polynesia—its conquest and occupation by brute Force.

Melville's response to the war whose nature, methods, masks, and results he saw in the South Seas is the source of virtually all in *Typee* and *Omoo* that foretells the workings of his mature poetic imagination: alertness to scenes and figures capable of communicating fundamental realities of human life in his time; sensitivity to ironies and inner contradictions indicative of the nature of the distorting codes of nineteenth-century civilization that are inimical to peaceful human relations; and a deep sense of what is beautiful in people, nature, and life in contrast to what is ugly or grotesque.

The young Melville wanted worldly success. Yet, exotic as are many of the experiences he included in his first two books, much as he spiced his accounts with dangers and dancing girls, and amenable as he was to making some changes to meet the wishes of his publishers, he still placed his great emphasis on the destructive effects of the imperialist and religious wars of conquest in the South Pacific, a theme that could not fail to alienate a large part of his potential public, as the following passage in *Typee* demonstrates he well knew: "As wise a man as Shakespeare has said, that the bearer of evil tidings hath but a losing office; and so I suppose will it prove with me" (xxvi, 198). We must be impressed by how strong a motive force, then as afterward, was his compulsion to voice through his art his abhorrence of the wars of "white civilized man."

Notes

1. *Typee* (Evanston, Ill: Northwestern Univ. Press and the Newberry Library, 1968). All references in the text will be to this edition. The emphasis in this quotation is mine. In subsequent references to this and other works of Melville in the text, the book form "(ii, 12)," or a slightly modified version of it, will be used to cite chapter and page numbers.
2. *Omoo* (Evanston, Ill.: Northwestern Univ. Press and the Newberry Library, 1968).
3. Van Wyck Brooks considered *Omoo* "a book of pure adventure" written in a "morning mood." Gordon Roper's "Historical Note" in the Northwestern edition of *Omoo* quotes other critics whose readings of *Omoo* are similar.

2.

The Unifying Force in the Shaping of *Mardi*

Awareness of Melville's powerful feeling against war irradiates the design partly hidden beneath the deluge of words and material in *Mardi* (1849). Without this awareness one might agree that Melville's third book is "a hash of adventure, romance, satire, and jejune philosophizing." [1] Or one might think of it as having organic form [2] but not as having evolved, by the time it was completed, a consciously conceived configuration. Yet *Mardi*'s large design, the natural outgrowth of its fundamental thought, reveals itself to be a remarkable conception reflecting Melville's exploration of the nineteenth-century world and its relation to infinite time and space. In the course of the book's transformation from a simple sequel to *Omoo* to a work of boldest experimentation,[3] Melville's imagination became not only alchemized but alchemizing; and not only did Polynesia give way to Mardi, metaphor of the world, but the work itself took on the form of the "great globe of globes" within the "endless sea" of the universe. Out of the "outer confines of creation," into and around the mid-nineteenth-century world, and back into the "outer ocean," man in his incarnation as white civilized man travels from birth to death in *Mardi*. By means of this voyage, Melville turned over in his mind the

13

world of his day and developed ideas about it that he had begun to think about in *Typee* and *Omoo*. Since to him that world was a warring world and white civilized man the animal shown by his wars to be the most ferocious on the face of the earth,[4] antiwar thinking inevitably became the guiding force in the new book—inspiring its contour; acting as a lodestar to its narrative; and creating a web of interrelationships among its myriad scenes, histories, songs, comic passages, and philosophical or social discussions.

Rereading *Mardi* with a sense of Melville's almost continuous consciousness of war in the world is a progression of enlightenments. First, reverberations of images, words, ideas, and types of incidents convey that there is an association in Melville's imagination of these crimes against Oro (*Mardi*'s name for a God synonymous with Life): murder; Cain's crime, which combines fratricide and denial of responsibility for the life of a brother; and war—the most magnified form of fratricide. *Omoo*'s axiomatic statement that war is the greatest of evils becomes *Mardi*'s indirect assertion that war is man's primal crime. Perception by the reader of the murder/fratricide/war association brings the realization that there is a tide in Melville's growing artistic imagination that carries the first third of the book, climaxing in the murder committed by Taji (upon whose brow the mark of Cain will later be visible) into the seemingly unrelated odyssey around Mardi. The unified fratricide/war theme is then seen to be the one that moves through the narrative, drawing with it the countless seemingly ill-assorted episodes and conversations, all of which are organically related in that they reflect a fratricidal world. It becomes apparent, then, that some incidents are in the mainstream while others are wanderings from the course: the former are those referred to before or after they occur, the memorable scenes essential to the development of the main theme of the book; the latter are those, usually brief, that Melville tacitly admits to be "expatiations" by the way in which he leads back from them to the main theme.[5] Reasons appear for the inclusion and placement of many songs and stories that would otherwise seem to have been written on the spur of the moment and never reconsidered. Boundaries between groups of episodes and discussions become visible. And at last *Mardi* emerges as the work of a large organizing intelligence and a unifying poetic imagination. That Melville felt he had, at least in part, achieved his evolved intentions concerning the shape of his book is confirmed by the writing experience of Lombardo, author of the Kostanza, *Mardi*'s fictional counterpart near the end (clxxx, 592–602). It is King Abrazza who never read the Kostanza who finds it "wild, unconnected, all episode." Its author, although he did not know in the beginning what his book would become but only plunged deeper and deeper into himself to find his way through the "baffling woods," in time saw the "whole boundless landscape" stretch before him and then began to work in earnest, acting as both critic and creator, until the "round world" emerged from "primal chaos."

Although the integrating force in *Mardi* is the association of murder, fratricide, and war, the main theme can be thought of simply as the antiwar theme. The association of Taji with Cain links Taji's story to the biblical one that symbolizes the beginning of war in the human family. The story of Taji's killing of the old Polynesian priest allegorizes the brute Force used by the "civilized" world to seize what it wants. The imagery in *Mardi* that depicts or reflects the mid-nineteenth-century world also shows war at the center of Melville's vision of it. Beneath him "the earth pulses and beats like a warrior's heart" (cxix, 367). "Mankind seems in arms" (clxiv, 541). All Mardi threatens to be "one conflagration" (cliii, 499). In the Antarctic there are "navies of icebergs,—warring worlds crossing orbits; their long icicles, projecting like spears to the charge" (cxix, 366). Recurring war symbols— sharks and spears, clouds and storms, meteors and volcanoes—are at the heart of Melville's imagination in *Mardi*. Above all, the title, *Mardi*, French for "Tuesday," and by derivation the day of Mars, is the name Melville chose for the world of his day. (A "man-of-war world" he would call it a year later in *White-Jacket.*)

Melville's view of the modern world and his desire to seek out its relation to the past and future of humanity are reflected in the design of *Mardi*. The work's shape and its unifying murder/fratricide/war theme can be visualized diagrammatically. Imagine three concentric circles surrounded by space on a marginless page; picture, too, a line moving from the outer space on the left through the common center and then out into the outer space on the right.

The line follows the westward course of the narrative. The unbordered outer area represents the infinite sea of space and time implied by the cosmic imagery in the beginning; by the "outer ocean" at the end; and by the way the star Arcturus in the last chapter leads back to the ship *Arcturion* in the first. (Since Melville's universe is curved, it is possible to sink into it in the west, like the sun, and arise again in the east.) The opening and close of *Mardi* thus form a setting for everything in between. The left-hand part of the first ring within the outer space presents symbolically the "deliverance" into historical time of the main character, who stands, in general, for man in his "blended" generations (iii, 12) and, in particular, for nineteenth-century man. In this region (24-200), the character reenacts man's primal crime, in a doomed attempt to capture his ideal of happiness by violent means. In the part of this ring situated on the right (650-54), symbolic man, failing still to see the connection between the ideal and the real and failing to renounce his crime, darts back into the universe. Like the outer space, this ring is a frame for whatever lies within it. The second inward ring signifies the "atmosphere" of Earth as seen by the five characters who tour Mardi. Its first part (201-464) contains the imaginary places Melville created; outstanding among these are Juam, the land with a history of fratricide and war; Diranda, island of the war games; and Maramma, where the sharks are sacred. The righthand part of this ring (556-649) climaxes in Serenia, the place that sums up the fratricidal essence of the rest of Mardi by contrast. The innermost circle stands for the "globe of globes" in 1848 (465-555). In this region the travelers find war, history of war, or threat of war everywhere. Since the narrative line passes twice through each zone around the mid-nineteenth-century world, once before and once after the tour of Earth, *Mardi* can be seen to be a sophisticated, complex and uniquely conceived "frame story" that is truly valid in that its settings and center express with integrity Melville's developing conceptions of the nature of the world and interrelationships within the universe.

Only one character travels the whole course, from outer ocean to outer ocean, birth to death. He is Taji who, like civilized man, reenacts the original sin, which to Melville is not that of Adam and Eve but that of Cain. In the first two chapters (3–10) he is a sailor on the whaling ship *Arcturion* where, on the symbolic level, he is nineteenth-century man about to be born, still in the sea of space and time, the "outer confines of creation," to which he will return in the end: his days are "endless and uneventful as cycles in space"; his hammock, like a pendulum, tells "centuries and ages"; the ocean rolls "illimitably." His shoving off from the ship is like a deliverance (vii, 25). He leaves the "maternal craft" (24) amid repeated cries of *"Man* overboard" (28; my emphasis). The tackle ropes tying the small boat into which he drops from the ship with a companion, the old sailor Jarl, have to be severed as an umbilical cord has to be cut.

The narrator, whom Melville leaves nameless at the beginning, and Jarl have been able to carry away with them in the small boat only what is needed for life. But eventually, on a nearly deserted brigantine, the young man, who at once assumes the role of master, takes on the equipment, and hence the implications of white civilized man: muskets, powder, bullets, cutlasses; and silks, nankeens, and trinkets to be offered as gifts. He also acquires a Polynesian named Samoa to work for him and finally, like Jarl, to die for him.

The tale of the sailor's murder of the old Polynesian priest Aleema and his carrying off of the girl Yillah is openly symbolic of civilized man's forcible appropriations and of his pretense that his purpose is noble. The young man's whiteness is highlighted as is, by means of his comment on the tattoo of "our Saviour" on Jarl's arm, the fact that he professes Christianity. He offers the Polynesians gifts and makes protestations of peace but invades their canoe carrying a cutlass, accompanied by Samoa with a knife, and backed up by Jarl who remains in the boat with muskets loaded. He briefly admits to himself that his real motives in murdering the priest are covered over with "a gracious pretense; concealing myself from myself." He beats down the thought (xliv, 140), and throughout the later narrative he flees his stabs of conscience. As he and his two-man crew sail off with Yillah, the sons of Aleema, javelins poised, follow the small whaling boat in their sacred canoe. All through *Mardi* they appear, always following, even into the endless sea—the fates whom the sailor has set in his own pursuit.

Everything in Yillah's description and story (xliii–lxiv, 136–95)

the chaplains in *White-Jacket* and *Billy Budd,* Maramma's Pontiffs serve the warmakers: they are on the "most friendly terms" with the "ravenous sharks" (already established in the paddle-chant as warmakers preying and slaying), "sociably bathing with them in the sea; permitting them to rub their noses against their priestly thighs."

> At the ordination of a Pontiff, the ceremony was not deemed complete, until embarking in his barge, he was saluted High Priest by three sharks drawing near; with teeth turned up, swimming beside his canoe.
>   These monsters were deified in Maramma; had altars there; it was deemed worse than homicide to kill one. "And what if they destroy human life?" say the Islanders, "are they not sacred?" (cviii, 334)

The last place visited before the travelers reach the "globe of globes," and in that sense an archway into it, is Diranda, land of the war games (cxxxvii–cxlii). That Melville intended this section to mark the archlike boundary separating the imaginary places in this part of the work from the sphere representing the 1848 world more precisely will be stressed when the opposite arc is reached, for he will again set the boundary as the travelers sail out of the waters of the inner sphere: "and all the lands that we had passed, since leaving Piko's shore of spears, were faded from the sight" (clxix, 556).

Through Diranda, the "land of clubs and javelins" where King Piko and King Hello rule, one in the East and one in the West of a single island, Melville communicates the idea of one world in which men have been killing each other. As the voyagers approach this quintessential place Media asks Yoomy to sing the battle-chant of Narvi. A development of the paddle-chant, it is a monstrous paean glorifying the butchery of war. Its grotesque diction and images, as indeed the unblinking ferocity of the whole Diranda section, is an index of Melville's horror at the whole idea of war. Like *White-Jacket* and *Israel Potter,* the Diranda section bluntly attacks the illusion that there is glory in warmaking. It reveals as accessories of the crime those priests, damsels, writers, and composers who let themselves be used to lure men to fight. Most responsible, however, are the people themselves, who unprotestingly go off to kill and be killed "at regular intervals." That rulers might be made powerless to conduct their games of war if there were strong opposition is conveyed by the effect of "the Despairer," a father driven mad by the death of his sons, who enters the arena shouting and threatening all, causing the kings to flee in terror. At the same moment that Piko and Hello are pursued by the father, Taji is pursued by the sons of Aleema. Their reappearance at this point is a reminder that Taji's murder of the Polynesian priest is not part of a personal story but a symbol of the wars of white civilized man that are as bloody as the games just witnessed and, like them, are conducted for the benefit of "kings."

On the globe representing Earth, histories of wars by "civilized" man, his present wars, and threats of war as "Judgment" are dominant on every continent: the two other great ills—slavery in Vivenza (the United States) and tyranny everywhere, with its accompanying poverty—are shown to have originated in, and to be maintained by, brute Force and to be the seed of future wars. Media, drunk, confesses, "Peace is War against all kings," to which Babbalanja replies, "Ay, ay, my lord, your royal order will endure, so long as men will fight. Break the spears, and free the nations" (clxiv, 541).

Logically the tour of the 1848 world starts in Dominora since nineteenth-century England, which it represents, best illustrates military might dominant in the world. Bello is King. Archbreeder of wars, he thrusts his spear everywhere outside his island, and he sends his warriors against Chartistlike protesters at home.

The chronicles of Verdanna (Ireland) are covered with blood. And in Porpheero (Europe) the past casts its shadows, and wars are erupting all over the continent. So the group heads for Vivenza to see if happiness is there.

For all her boasts and even her "better aspect," Vivenza has the same ills as Porpheero and more besides. She has appropriated the land of the indigenous people and has all but exterminated them. The stripes of the national flag being hoisted to the top of her Temple of Freedom correspond to the red stripes on the back of the slave raising the banner. The lunatic Alanno (inspired by Senator

William Allen, expansionist and spokesman for President Polk during the war against Mexico) brags of the invincibility of "this ineffable land" and tries to stir up a war with Dominora; he wishes to be heard "from one end of this great and gorgeous land to its farthest zenith; ay, to the uttermost diameter of its circumference" (clviii, 517), his ridiculous rhythm and diction expressing Melville's mockery of chauvinism. Vivenza's territorial expansion parallels Dominora's empire building: her "great chieftain," though no king, has done an imperial thing by precipitating her into an undeclared war (the so-called Mexican War). Her purchases of territory from other nations are enforced by "the spear." In an anonymous scroll in which diverse views are turned over, Melville presents an opinion with which none of the travelers disagrees, that Vivenza should remember the fate of Romara (ancient republican Rome) when her "terrible king-tigers came," and she acted like the "bloody hawk" (clxi, 526).

In Vivenza's South (clxii) slavery, the sin that "puts out the sun at noon" and "parches all fertility," portends war: "These South Savannahs may yet prove battle-fields." Through Yoomy, Melville expresses the part of himself that sympathizes with any effort to end the "vast enormity," but accompanying this feeling is his horror at the thought of war; the conflict is an early sign of the tension at the heart of *Battle-Pieces*.

Sailing South from Vivenza the seekers for a place where happiness dwells come to a cluster of green (Caribbean) islands whose peace is gone; they have been appropriated by the rulers of Dominora and Porpheero, and Vivenza lusts after them. Along the shore of Kolumbo of the South, the group considers the wars always in progress on that continent, and Babbalanja predicts that the people will soon have tyrants over them again if they cleave to war.

The last three chapters in the inner sphere of *Mardi* form a unit devoted largely to the theme that greed for "gold" is the main cause of the destruction of life and what is good in it. The first sets the tone: actual gold hunters kill each other. The second tells of the isles in the Pacific where exploiters from the outside world have brought death: "On ye, the nations prey like bears that gorge themselves with honey" (clxvii, 550). The third sweeps around the remaining areas of the globe. The conversation (clxviii, 551–52) as the group nears Orienda (the Orient) could serve as the text for a musical composition for four voices; its recitativo style following an introduction about cymbals, drums, psalteries, and music makes it virtually certain that Melville thought of it in this way. In a series of apostrophes to Orienda, in which images of light and night play an important part, the composition blends the themes of aggression for profit, of murder within the human family, of war as fratricide, of the culture of the East as the ancestor of the best culture of the West but now destroyed by the West, and of the role of Maramma's priests whose pious voices speak in vain, since they come from clouds of war. In the finale, Babbalanja warns: "Seed sown by spears but seldom springs; and harvests reaped thereby are poisoned by the sickle's edge"; again, an outstanding though brief section ends with a reminder of Judgment coming as a natural consequence of human acts. As the voyagers pass the western shore of Hamora (Africa) from which Vivenza's slaves were "torn," Yoomy voices the same conception: "Poor land! curst of man, not Oro! . . . Oh tribe of Hamo! thy cup of woe so brims, that soon it must overflow upon the land which holds ye thralls." That Melville is prophesying war of great violence as Judgment for the United States is at once confirmed in metaphor: a storm comes down, bursting "its thousand bombs"; lightning flashes; the billows smite as they rear; and Babbalanja speaks for all in this climactic prophecy: "Thus, oh Vivenza! retribution works! Though long delayed, it comes at last—Judgment, with all her bolts."

The seekers for Yillah sail out of the inner globe to be again in the realm of imaginary places, all but one of them representative of the 1848 world. They see three such imaginary places before they arrive in Serenia. In Hooloomooloo, where the inhabitants, all crippled, think themselves at the summit of human perfection, the former king's body is now indistinguishable from that of the pet chimpanzee buried with him, and the Hooloomoolooans fear the monument they have been erecting (the structure of civilization) may commemorate an ape. The scene in the woods of Doxodox, renowned in Mardi for his wisdom, reflects civilized man's worship of handed-down empty words incapable of tackling the real problems of life. Doxodox has a vocabulary of concocted terms in the field of logic; he knows his "Sumptions" and his "*A*ssumptions" but of the Shark-Syllogism about which Babbalanja questions him he is ignorant and scornful, that is, he knows nothing about the links Melville has been establishing among sharks, warmakers and churchmen or about the harm they bring, and he does not care to devote his thinking, which has nothing to do with the world, to such mundane matters.

The last place visited (before Serenia) casts an arching light back to Odo, the place from which the voyagers embarked, for Bonovona depicts in sum what Odo prefigures. The near identity of these islands and their kings prepares the way for the eventual contrast between Media as he was and Media as he will be after he visits Serenia, for King Abrazza of Bonovona is essentially Media as he was at the start. He has the outlook of those who enjoy power in a world they rule by force, Melville giving "enjoyment" the form of eating, drinking, laughing. Though his island is largely "overcast with shadows" and plaintive notes issue forth from its groves, "heartless" Abrazza turns his back on its shadowy side and with a placid smile pities the sufferers, just as he pities those he sends down into shark-infested waters so that treasure may be laid at his feet. Armed guards pace his groves, and spears are used against the poor who seek to present petitions. He is a carefree bachelor, one who, as Babbalanja defines *bachelor,* sends out into battle (into shark-infested waters) "brigades and battalions" of other men's sons. Over Bonovona, too, a cloud of Judgment threatens: an enormous man looms out of the throng of petitioners, "a pent storm on his brow," muttering about a dark time that is coming.

At last the travelers sail from the violent swell of a night storm to a peaceful golden dawn as they near Serenia, the place that contrasts with all they have seen, where Alma (Christ) is restored to his original meaning and men strive to live together in peace and brotherhood. The section (clxxxvi–clxxxix) flashes its contrasting light back on the "shade upon shade" of Maramma and on the world of Maramma-sanctioned crimes where shadows are everywhere and "true brotherhood there is none." Although the Serenians do not proclaim faith in Alma, they try to live according to his words; to them, acts are the "truthful symbols" of belief. For each of the travelers except Taji the stay in Serenia is the turning point in his understanding and story. Mohi sees the true lesson of history in the words of the old man who explains the life of the Serenians. Yoomy feels the old man's words to be poetry, since poetry is truth. Media renounces his claim to demigodship and resolves that no more will dismal cries be heard from Odo's groves. Especially effective in the narrative development is the strong impression Serenia makes on Babbalanja, since he has been the one most hostile to Alma's faith because of the wrongs committed in its name. In a vision Babbalanja sees Mardi from space, and the world is as if re-created: "Like a spark new-struck from flint, soon Mardi showed afar. It glowed within a sphere, which seemed, in space, a bubble, rising from vast depths to the sea's surface" (clxxx-viii, 636). In the morning he tells the others he will remain in Serenia, but only until he becomes wiser; then he will be Alma's and the world's. He urges them to use their talents to help in the re-creation of Mardi. He tells Yoomy to remember that nations are but names and to take all Mardi for his home. He enjoins Media to return home to Odo, where war has broken out, and to improve life there: "Let no man weep, that thou may'st laugh." And Taji should give up his obsession with a "phantom": there is, Babbalanja has discovered in his vision, no transcendent beatitude, as there is no final knowledge. Taji should know that he can find in his heart all he seeks. He advises him to stay in Serenia and be safe; for vengeance cannot exist there. But, in contrast to Media, Taji does not renounce his claims to being a demigod above the concerns of suffering humanity.

Throughout the tour of Mardi there have been reminders of Taji's separate story: at intervals the avengers have appeared in pursuit, and in one such interlude he has confessed his crime to the others and has said he would repeat it for the same gain. In appearances accompanying those of Aleema's sons, the sirens of a mysterious Queen Hautia have come to lure him to her. He has felt inwardly stabbed when Yoomy has translated their flower messages, since they call out to his conscience. Each time he has turned them away. But now (cxcii), as the path of the narrative moves out again to be in the sphere of the design that contains his separate story, he consents to visit their queen, for "in some mysterious way seemed Yillah and Hautia connected" (cxci, 643). He has an opportunity to see the connection, but his eyes are "frozen shut."

Just as everything in the description of Yillah points to her being an abstract ideal isolated from contact with the world, so everything in the story and in the description of Hautia reveals her as the concrete world in which the abstract must reside if it is not to be merely a "phantom." Taji thinks that he sees Yillah deep in Hautia's eyes, but he turns away. His Yillah is an escape from the world, not something far within it. Not for him is the thought voiced by Babbalanja on seeing the gold hunters that it is vain to snatch at happiness: "Of that we may not pluck and eat. It is the fruit of our own toilsome planting; slow it grows, nourished by many tears, and all our earnest tendings. Yet ere it ripen, frosts may nip;—and then, we plant again; and yet again. Deep . . . deep, true treasure lies; deeper than all Mardi's gold, rooted to Mardi's axis. But unlike gold it lurks in every soil—all Mardi over" (clxvi, 547). But for Taji, who takes what he wants by force, no such advice is welcome. Instead, he compulsively follows his phantom, "white and vaguely Yillah," into the endless sea. His escape from deeper knowledge of the world, which would require the renunciation of his crime, is conducted in characteristic fashion. He seizes from Mohi and Yoomy the boat in which they come to rescue him and darts into the outer ocean, leaving them to swim for their lives. Like Ahab, whom he resembles in rigidity, he is last seen as a weapon: he darts into the outer ocean like an arrow following an undeviating path. The sons of Aleema pursue him still, Melville's last reminder that Taji chose his fate when he killed the old priest. In "madness" he committed that murder, and in a mad rage he destroys life again, this time his own: "Now, I am my own soul's emperor; and my first act is abdication!" Readers who believe that Melville identifies with Taji think that he finds Taji's pursuit of the unattainable heroic, but it is the sailor's *soul* that is relinquished, and, ironically, he who rejected the indivisibility of the ideal and the physical in life recognizes it, though unconsciously, at the moment of death, abandoning simultaneously his bodily existence and his soul.

So arrow follows arrow into the outer ocean. Is this the inevitable pattern of human history as Melville in *Mardi* sees it? At first, the concluding sentence seems to say that it is: "And thus pursuers and pursued flew on, over an endless sea." But the reader who looks back on *Mardi* in the round thinks of much that seems to say otherwise: Media, Babbalanja, Yoomy, and Mohi have changed, and so have their conceptions of the areas of thought they represent; there has been a "low undertone" (cxlii, 454) throughout the book affirming that a seed of brotherhood and peace in humanity's heart may someday germinate and grow if tended; Babbalanja's vision has given a glimpse of a new Mardi, though it shows itself "afar"; and Taji has had the possibility of staying in Serenia where the arrows of the pursuers cannot enter—the possibility of living like a Serenian, no more a human weapon. But from the time of his delivery into the world of Melville's day to his self-fated end he has not changed and does not want to change. When he arises again in a new generation, will his life story take a different turn in a world in which more creative concepts in philosophy, poetry, history, and government may affect man's consciousness? Closer examination of the last sentence of *Mardi* shows that it does not describe the pursuit as endless, only the sea. *Mardi* gives no more final answer about what future is to be anticipated than does any other Melville work. What the book elaborates is the question plainly formulated on its first page, in the one-line second paragraph that Melville must have added late in the evolution of *Mardi*, when its shape was clear: "But whence, and whither wend ye, mariners?"

Since the answer is left for us mariners in our "blended" generations to pursue, the "destiny yet unaccomplished" that the early story of Yillah prophesied for her—that she will well up at last in an "inland" fountain in Oroolia—never materializes in the narrative. But the happiness man seeks, which is inseparable from the world and its needs, may well up at last in his heart, which is where Oro must be in terms of the work's imagery. That Melville's imagination conceived the heart of humanity as potentially creative and happy is borne out in *Moby-Dick*, in which the deep "inland" in Ishmael is the peaceful part of his being (lxxxvii) and humanity's inner "Tahiti" is full of peace and joy.

So the inner and outer worlds are closely interrelated by the end of *Mardi*. The heart of white, civilized, modern man (Taji) has been uncaring about the world and human life. He has killed and is prepared to kill again. As long as man remains unchanged—his patterns of thought and deed rigid—so long must a self-created vengeance pursue him. But, Lombardo says, "Somewhere Mardi has a mighty heart—*that* struck, all the isles shall resound!" (clxxx, 600). To this still undiscovered "inland" heart, which turns out to be the center of all the concentric spheres in the design of *Mardi*, Melville addressed his first experimental work of the poetic imagination.

Notes

1. Willard Thorp, "Herman Melville," in *Literary History of the United States,* ed. Robert E. Spiller et al. (New York: Macmillan, 1963), p. 449.
2. Nathalia Wright, "Form as Function in Melville," *PMLA,* 67 (1952), 330–40.
3. See the "Historical Note" by Elizabeth S. Foster in *Mardi* (Evanston, Ill.: Northwestern Univ. Press and The Newberry Library, 1970), pp. 657–81. Page references to *Mardi* in my text are to this edition.
4. *Typee* (Evanston, Ill.: Northwestern Univ. Press and The Newberry Library, 1968), Ch. xvii, p. 125.
5. For example, the digression on smoking pipes ends with the idea that the pipe and the sword are the eloquent symbols (of peace and war, respectively) summing up life; the visit to the antiquary concludes: "The microscope disgusts us with our Mardi, and the telescope sets us longing for some other world."

3.

White-Jacket's Center: "So long as a man-of-war exists. . . ." [1]

all hopeless *prisoners like myself*; all under martial law . . . *all in one uniform.*

—*White-Jacket*, xlii, 174

"*Jacket* do you call it!" cried a captain of the hold. "Why not call it a *white-washed man-of-war schooner?*"

—*White-Jacket*, xlvii, 202

Two passages in earlier Melville works point to the center around which *White-Jacket* (1850) revolves. When in *Mardi* Babbalanja says to King Media, "Ay, ay, my lord, your royal order will endure, so long as men will fight. Break the spears, and free the nations," [2] the statement predicts *White-Jacket*'s focal conception that the tyranny on the man of war *Neversink* stems from the fact that the ship's prime purpose is war; [3] it is also an early expression of the disarmament theme suggested in the image of the *Neversink* (counterpart of the world of war Earth) with "her guns hoisted out—her powder-magazine, shot-lockers, and armories discharged —till not one vestige of a fighting thing [is] left in her, from furthest stem to uttermost stern" (xciii, 396). Similarly, when *Omoo*'s footnote declares, "War being the greatest of evils, all its accessories necessarily partake of the same character," [4] that generalization, with its emphasis on war as the primary ill, anticipates *White-Jacket*'s demonstration throughout that in a ship—or world—oriented toward the "greatest of evils," the whole of the war machine is inevitably nutritive of evil and inimical to good. The documentary and imaginative elements of *White-Jacket* combine to convey that as "the very object of a man-of-war, as its name implies, is to fight the very battles so naturally averse to the seamen; so long as a man-of-war exists, it must ever remain a picture of much that is tyrannical and repelling in human nature" (xlix, 208); whereas some of a man-of-war's evils are generated by the naval code, "others are absolutely organic to a Navy establishment . . . incurable, except when they dissolve with the body they live in" (lxxxix, 375). It is Melville's feeling against war, which he sees as providing the basis for tyranny, and not a feeling against tyranny per se,[5] that accounts for *White-Jacket*'s dynamics: it interrelates the assorted chapters and incidents, inspires the imagery, influences the general narrative form and direction, and unites the personal and documentary aspects of the book. For although it is true that, to a large degree, *White-Jacket* is a patchwork of bits and pieces, many of them taken from other men's writings and refashioned (as Charles R. Anderson and then Howard P. Vincent have richly demonstrated),[6] the patches and the new pieces create one overall picture of a warship with bristling broadsides [7] on whose deck the captain, with the Articles of War in one hand, brandishes a cat-o'-nine-tails with the other, to keep the men at their guns; the chaplain lends the sanction of his religion to the scene; the "professor" holds up a cannonball to signify the world; and the narrator (whose constricting jacket—in its most important qualities and effects—symbolizes the "uniform" in which all the common sailors are imprisoned) both observes and feels the scene. The documentary account and the personal one, far from being disparate pieces clumsily sewn together, are necessary to each other and to the whole picture. Each reflects the other and brings out the other's ideas and poetic concepts. The documentary account presents the outer view of what exists in a "man-of-war world" (the phrase recurs regularly throughout the book); the personal story presents the subjective, or "inside" [8] experience of what it means to be held down in that constantly death-threatening environment.

This view of *White-Jacket*, a departure from convention in that the antiwar theme is held to be primary rather than subordinate, involves an interpretation of the personal story's main symbol far different from the one generally accepted in the critical commu-

nity.[9] According to that other view, the jacket has a purely personal significance—"isolation" on the part of its wearer, resulting
from what is thought to be his "refusal to participate in the ordinary life of humanity." [10] Now it is true that the narrator (though
with no special emphasis or imaginative expression) speaks of himself as, for example, "somewhat aloof from" (somewhat distanced
from?) "the mass of seamen on board the Neversink" (xlii, 174).
But in the book as a whole, as in the larger passage in which the
foregoing remark occurs, the great weight of the material White-
Jacket treats, as well as the feelings he most intensely and authen-
tically reports as his, conveys his "common sympathy," his sense of
identification with the mass of men on the man of war, all prisoners "like myself" (174). He is not, in his thoughts, alienated from
the ordinary life of humanity; *that* is in fact his main concern. Nor
is he isolated in the narrative. The reader should take note of the
number and variety of men who confide in him and to whom he
listens and ask: why, if it is not to stress White-Jacket's feeling of
human responsibility, Melville has him attend to his sick messmate
Shenly in the airless, stinking ship's hospital, and then to his dead
body (even saving it from a traditional mutilation), in a way that
is far beyond the call of duty or of ordinary easy sympathy. The
substance of the work as a whole, as exemplified by the Shenly
story, contradicts the idea that the jacket is the symbol of anything
like childish egoism. Close analysis of the personal story of the
sailor and his jacket and then of the related documentary-poetic
account of the *Neversink* confirms that the man-of-war metaphor
and the jacket metaphor concur with each other and that Melville's antiwar feeling is at the heart of the work—a fact of which he
regularly reminds the reader by including the words "in a man-of-
war" in forty of his chapter titles.

The jacket story, which is minimal in terms of events, is sturdy
as a co-conductor of the conception that man needs to break out of
the straitjacket of war and of "essentially" cruel martial discipline
(lxxvii, 328). The narrator is known only as White-Jacket, the absence of a personal and family name giving him the representative
significance of any ordinary sailor on a warship, where numbers
and not names direct men to their stations. The two most important sections of the jacket story—the first telling how the narrator

comes to be forced to wear the monstrous garment and the second how he is liberated from it—enclose, as in brackets, his account of his voyage in a man of war.

In all likelihood written after the book began to evolve in its present form, the two-page first chapter is a Melville prelude in which the theme of the work is predicted. It acquaints the reader with the jacket and hints at what it will signify. It is not "*very* white," say the opening words, hinting at once that it is not a glorious, shining coat. It is "stiff," ill conceived, ill fitting, and padded with old discardable material. Not only does it not serve its intended purpose of protection against cold and wet; it is at all times a "burden" to wear, and when it is soaked it weighs the narrator down like an anchor. It is not something he chooses to sport; the wearing of it is imposed upon him when he finds himself returning from the Pacific (as did Melville on the frigate *United States*); he has no warm coat, and none is available from the ship's stores, so that he must concoct one. (That he did not have the grotesque jacket earlier also must rule it out as a symbol of "psychological infantilism," [11] a trait one does not suddenly develop.) He wants to make the jacket waterproof by painting it. (As it turns out, black is the color he has in mind, so one cannot logically draw psychoanalytical conclusions from its whiteness.) But the captain of the paint room refuses point-blank to provide what he needs. Thus, concentratedly, Melville hints in his prelude at the inhumanity White-Jacket is to find inherent in a ship, or world, whose object, even in times between hostilities, is war. Although such a world is presumably designed for the defense of its population, it does not provide its "People" with protection; on the contrary, it imposes upon them hardships and menaces to life.

As a result of the tone-setting callousness of the captain of the paint room, the narrator must continue to wear the unpainted jacket. Until the future moment, openly foretold in the first chapter, when the jacket will come near to being his white shroud, it is, like the man of war, an object that threatens death to whoever is enclosed in it. It is a source of humiliation to him as a human being, a thing the ordinary sailors, including White-Jacket himself, blast; at the mess, when all the members, except one, offer to leave with him if he is driven out, the young sailor distinguishes between himself and his jacket, saying to the gunner's mate who wants him gone: "Blast my jacket you may, and I'll join you in *that;* but don't blast *me*" (333). The jacket sticks to him, not he to it. Melville has the narrator think of tossing it overboard, but feel that it will spread itself in wait for him at the bottom of the sea—very likely in order that Melville can later show that it must be "pierced through and through" if it is to be no future threat.

At one point the sailor tries to rid himself of it at the ship's auction. This seems mainly a documentary scene, and a funny one, but it is, above all, a symbolic episode highly important in the interaction between the account of the ship and the mirroring personal story. There are no bids made for the jacket: the common sailors are, one might say, "naturally averse" and filled with an "incurable antagonism" to it, just as they are said to be toward war, in the chapter that follows on the heels of this one and another that is a related digression. Not only are there no takers; the men reject the jacket with strong comments, in the course of which a captain of the hold spells out (unconsciously on his part) the poetic association in Melville's imagination: "*Jacket* do you call it! Why not call it a *white-washed man-of-war schooner?*" (xlvii, 202; the first emphasis is Melville's, the second mine). After this equation is made, Melville speaks through the auctioneer: "No one will give me a bid, then? Very good; here, shove it aside. Let's have something else there" (203).

The "something else" Melville would like to have replace the man-of-war world is implied in his description of the social atmosphere in the "top," the environment symbolically above that of the decks of the *Neversink*. It is a free and peaceful place where the men are "brothers one and all." From his "airy perch" White-Jacket can "literally" look down upon the men "among the guns" (iv, 15) and can get a "bird's eye" (xii, 47) view of the man-of-war world below.

The concluding event in the jacket story conveys again, this time with great poetic power, that the strange item of attire concocted by Melville is an analogue (in a suggestive, not a mechanical way) of the kind of world that humanity, if it is to survive and live creatively, must "shove aside" and replace with "something else." Chapter xcii, entitled "The last of the Jacket" (which comes di-

rectly before the chapter telling of the last of the *Neversink,*) is a
dramatic, sensuous [12] expression of what *White-Jacket* implies all
along: man must choose between life and the unnecessary death
(or the death-in-life) inevitable in a man-of-war world. *Life* and
death—synonyms, in this book, of *peace* and *war*—are counterposed
throughout, but nowhere is the contrast and choice so sharp as in
the climactic scene in which the jacket takes the sailor down into
the depths of the ocean, a unique scene in fiction, whose essence
must almost certainly have been transmitted to the imagination of
Bible reader Melville by the passage in Deuteronomy in which
God places life and death before man and urges him to choose life.
The event that ends in the narrator's liberation from the jacket
coincides with the arrival at last of the *Neversink* near port. This is
not a mere matter of finishing off two lines of narrative as a book
nears completion. Once more the connection between the jacket
and the man of war is signaled, the event being both introduced by
a statement that the frigate is now near the Capes of Virginia and
immediately followed by a postscript that starts the next chapter:
"And now that the white jacket has sunk to the bottom of the sea,
and the blessed Capes of Virginia are believed to be broad on our
bow . . . our five hundred souls are fondly dreaming of home"
(395). Again the jacket and the man of war are linked. What is
more, it is all five hundred souls ("all in one uniform"), not only
White-Jacket, who can dream of home now that the white jacket
has sunk to the bottom of the sea. "The last of the Jacket," Chapter xcii, tells how the narrator chooses Life and how he delivers
himself from his imprisoning jacket—sinking it forever, with the
help of the crew. The incident begins with his fall from the yardarm when the ship plunges suddenly, and he, since he has been
leaning over, is pitched head foremost through the air. The heavy
skirts of his jacket fall around his head and muffle him. Ten thousand pounds of shot seem to be pulling him down. As he sinks into
the sea and is held there by his anchor of a jacket, he does not
know whether he is dead or still dying. All at once some "fashion-
less form" of life brushes his side, "the thrill of being alive again
tingled in my nerves, and the strong shunning of death shocked me
through." At first he hangs, "vibrating in the mid-deep," but the
"life-and-death poise" passes and he finds himself slowly ascending; then, his head no longer muffled, he sees a glimmer of light.

He is soon at the surface, able to breathe. On the ship hundreds of seamen are madly tossing ropes and hammocks to save him, but he is so far out he must swim to reach what they are throwing. He cannot swim, however, because he is "pinioned" by the jacket (as a bird is pinioned to restrict its flight). He must free himself of it if he is not to be drawn down again; he tries to tear it off, but the strings are tied tight. Then, "I whipped out my knife, that was tucked at my belt, and ripped my jacket straight up and down, as if I were ripping open myself. With a violent struggle I then burst out of it, and was free." The straitjacket in which he has been enclosed so long that it has come to seem an inescapable part of himself has been shed. But since it must be made incapable of enclosing him at some future time, it must be destroyed, and not by White-Jacket alone. Melville, therefore, does not make the sailor's individual shedding of it be the last of the jacket. White-Jacket watches it, and the impression is conveyed that if this object (which could better be called a man-of-war schooner) had had to be named by White-Jacket, he would have thought of it, also, as "Neversink." Now he adjures it to sink; and, sped on its way by the crew, at last it does:

> Sink! sink! oh shroud! thought I: sink forever! accursed jacket that thou art!
>
> "See that white shark!" cried a horrified voice from the taffrail; "he'll have that man down his hatchway! Quick! the *grains!* the *grains!*"
>
> The next instant that barbed bunch of harpoons pierced through and through the unfortunate jacket, and swiftly sped down with it out of sight. (394)

So life has been chosen over death; "Neversink" has been transformed into "Sink forever!" And three things have been brought into close imaginative correspondence: the imprisoning jacket that has almost carried the sailor to death; the man of war *Neversink* that the whole of *White-Jacket* invokes to "sink forever"; and the shark, Melville's symbol of warmaking, most clearly defined in *Mardi*.[13]

Now that the narrator is freed of the anchoring jacket (and of the idea that he is doomed to wear it eternally), and now that cable and anchor of the *Neversink* are also all clear (as the title of the next chapter phrases it), he is free to resume a personal name and life and to perform "the office imposed" upon him, that is, to write of what he has learned of life in a man-of-war world. Although he is sure that his book will subject him to the pillory in the minds of some, he is supported by what "God" [14] has given him, by which we can understand him to mean his experience, his talent, and his task. (White-Jacket's references to God throughout the book serve to emphasize the utter contrast between what religious—and especially Christian—principles are supposed to be and those that do actually guide the man-of-war world.) The truth that has long been "glazed over" (lxxxix, 375) about the whitewashed man-of-war world must, White-Jacket feels, be painted by him, though it be as ugly as was the head of Medusa to the ancient artist moved by *his* god (Jove) to depict it (xci, 386).

Once the reader becomes aware of Melville's association of the jacket and the man of war, he sees that the jacket story enriches the remainder of the work, brings out its essential poetic overtones, and illuminates the reason for Melville's choice of material. For example, Melville's image of White-Jacket "pinioned" in the sea suddenly lights the compelling poetic reason for Jack Chase's earlier remark, as Shenly's body is committed to the deep: "Look aloft. See that bird! it is the spirit of Shenly" (lxxxi, 342). Shenly's spirit, free of the pinioning man-of-war world, can now soar. With that idea planted, Melville can then lift it, in the reader's mind, to a new plane in "The last of the Jacket." Whereas Shenly's liberation comes only with death, White-Jacket becomes free in life. He will soar in this world by telling the truth of his experience and stirring his readers to wonder how the world can strip itself of the jacketing machinery of war. (Decades later the same bird image will reappear, with closely related antiwar significance, in *Billy Budd:* [15] Billy, in the scene of his execution, is a "pinioned figure" whose motion is ruled by the motion of "a great ship ponderously cannoned"—as White-Jacket is ruled until his release; Billy's last words are like the melody of "a singing bird on the point of launching from the twig." [16])

Conversely, the documentary-poetic portion of *White-Jacket* enriches the personal story, providing the necessary detailed evidence that war and war machinery drag men down. More complex in that it intermixes fact and fiction, the account of life on the *Neversink* gives the single-line, purely symbolic jacket story a three-dimensional corporeality.

Fundamental to his vision of life on the *Neversink* is Melville's lifetime conception that contemporary civilization is characterized, at bottom, by what *Billy Budd* calls "the abrogation of everything but brute Force." [17] The Articles of War resemble the Martial Law of which Sir Matthew Hale said that it was "in truth and reality, no law" (lxxii, 303). Such Articles are very nearly alike in all the "foremost states of Christendom," so the American document, threatening the common sailor with death at every turn, "indirectly becomes an index to the true condition of the present civilization of the world" (lxx, 293). White-Jacket calls the Articles of War Earth's "domineering code" ("The End," 399).

Now, the idea that brute Force or the threat of it is the essential means by which the foremost civilized nations have gained dominion in the world is no new understanding that the nineteenth century needed Melville to reveal, and he assumes it to be generally understood. But *White-Jacket* does offer a powerful original insight: that brute Force is also the essential means by which the foremost nations of the world compel their own "People" to wage war. The brutal flogging in the navy, to which Melville devotes so much space and passion, is, on the symbolic level of *White-Jacket,* the striking visualization of this internal brute Force. It dramatizes the idea continually put forward expositorily in *White-Jacket* that a population (not faced with invasion) must be whipped into war. For the common sailor has nothing to gain, says Chapter xlix, entitled "Rumors of a War, and how they were received by the Population of the Neversink," which explains that the common sailors "almost to a man" abhor the idea of going into battle. The Articles compel the ordinary sailor to fight "like a hired murderer . . . by digging his grave before his eyes if he hesitates" (lxxiv, 314): the purpose behind forcing the men to assemble round the capstan monthly to hear the Articles read is to instill terror; the phrase "Shall suffer death" booms in their ears "like the intermitting discharge of artillery" (lxx, 293).

One special phrase is a constantly recurring (subliminal) visual reminder of the underlying reality that the lives of the men on the *Neversink* are ruled by the fact that the ship serves what *Billy Budd* calls "the purpose attested by the cannon." [18] In scene after scene in his man-of-war world, Melville places common sailors "between the guns"—as so many years later in *Billy Budd* he will paint the young sailor, on the eve of his execution, "between the two guns." The phrase first appears in *White-Jacket* when, in the second chapter, Melville implies a comparison between the animals, penned up on deck waiting to be slaughtered to feed the appetites of the officers, and the common sailors, eating their poor food, penned up "between the guns." From then on, the phrase is, for the reader who begins consciously to note it, a continual clear refrain. He knows from the content of each scene in which the phrase appears that Melville is implying that the evils of each situation stem from the fact that men are imprisoned by guns, that those guns need to be stripped, as they finally are in the dramatic picture of the *Neversink* with no vestige of a fighting thing left in her.

Another memorable picture in *White-Jacket* also expresses the wish for a world free of war, the imagined scene of the "Judgment-day of the whole world's men-of-war," in which White-Jacket's God of peace and creation is almost visible hovering over all the flagships in history assembled at anchor in the great Bay of Rio. And the narration of the end of the voyage turns out, on close reading, to be a dream of the end of war itself: the brother band of topmen have trained the last gun; blown the last match; seen the last man tossed to the sharks; heard the last death-threatening Article of War (xciii, 396; remember that the many uses of the word *last* in the whole concluding section start with the chapter title announcing the last of the jacket).

White-Jacket sees the ideal of peace as within the powers of man to achieve—if he values it. He believes that each man in his heart fashions his own god, of war or of peace; that each mortal casts his vote for what he will to rule the world; that each human being has a voice that helps to shape eternity (lxxv, 320–21). Although the language he uses is grandiloquent—a fact that has made some critics question that the ideas are also Melville's—the above-mentioned conceptions are outstanding among those Melville will bring to life in *Moby-Dick*. Nor do we need to depend on White-Jacket's rhetoric to see that Melville himself expresses them in the art of *White-Jacket*.

As an outstanding example of Mellville's own expression of these ideas, let us take the ways in which Melville brings to life the idea that the *voice* is capable of shaping events, even of making the difference between life and death, good and evil, the dignity of man and his degradation. If more human beings followed the example of those "redeeming" men on the *Neversink* who speak up in the interests of the "People," the "thing called Fate"—Melville implies in some of the most dramatic scenes in *White-Jacket*—would be different. In each of these scenes the human voice, in various embodiments, triumphs over the tyranny of the man-of-war world. Each reveals Melville's way of creating symbolic events, or of so reworking events written up by others [19] that they, too, have symbolic significance.

The first of these scenes (xxvi, 104–9) occurs fairly early in the narrative, when the ship must round Cape Horn in a gale. Captain Claret (like Ahab) gives orders that would result in the destruction of ship and crew. "Hard *up* the helm," he shouts, his choice being to fly from the gale. But Mad Jack, the lieutenant who must have entered the world with a "speaking-trumpet" in his mouth (viii, 33), gives contrary orders, "Hard *down*—hard *down,* I say, and be damned to you!" Mad Jack is a man who knows that flying into the gale, "though attended with more appalling appearances, is, in reality, the safer [way]" (xxvii, 110). Thanks to him all lives are saved. The captain does not dare invoke the Articles of War or even reprimand this lieutenant, whose readiness to face the captain's fury (paralleling his readiness to face the fury of the gale) is, in every sense, victorious. His voice countermanding the captain's orders is one of the most memorable things in *White-Jacket*.

The second "speaking up" scene is the one in which White-Jacket is arraigned at the mast (lxvii, 277–81), about to be flogged for not answering to a number he has not been told is one of his. Outraged at the assault the flogging would be to his human dignity, he is ready to hurl the captain and himself to death in the sea. Then, against almost all precedent, Colbrook, corporal of marines, speaks up for him. "Seldom or never before had a marine dared to speak to the captain of a frigate in behalf of a seaman at the mast. But . . . the captain, though astounded, did not in any way reprimand him." Jack Chase, first captain of the top, "spokesman" for the men when they are denied liberty in Rio, and White-Jacket's special friend, takes heart and also speaks up. What follows reveals Melville's conception of man's "Fate" as something about which humanity has a voice. Melville's emphasis here is perhaps to show the irony of the captain's granting a release that has been wrested from him—for again the speaking up is successful:

> Captain Claret looked from Chase to Colbrook, and from Colbrook to Chase—one the foremost man among the seamen, the other the foremost man among the soldiers—then all round upon the packed and silent crew, and, as if a slave to Fate, though supreme Captain of a frigate, he turned to the First Lieutenant, made some indifferent remark, and saying to me *you may go,* sauntered aft into his cabin; while I, who, in the desperation of my soul, had but just escaped being a murderer and a suicide, almost burst into tears of thanksgiving where I stood. (281)

The human voice speaks most eloquently in the simple but determined words of old Ushant, the seaman whose term of office has expired. In spite of merciless floggings and being kept in irons "between the guns," he refuses to have his beard cut to a newly prescribed uniform length (lxxxvi–vii, 363–67). Insofar as the other men, who first refuse and then obey, are concerned, the incident has its humorous aspects, but Melville's treatment of Ushant is utterly serious. The old man's resistance to the tyranny of the captain, who says his orders "must be obeyed," is expressed in a low, tremulous tone. (Melville here echoes his idea in *Mardi*,[20] that there is in man, and has been since Mardi began, a beautiful low undertone like the one heard in the voices of some singers and poets.) "My beard is my own," Ushant says. "Captain Claret, you may flog me, if you will; but, sir, in this one thing I can *not* obey you." In the end, Ushant's resistance is also a triumph: the last view of him being rowed ashore from the *Neversink,* "amid the unsuppressible cheers of all hands," is a "glorious conquest over the Conqueror himself." He indirectly expresses Melville's idea in *White-Jacket* that the orders of the captains of the man-of-war world must not always be obeyed; the People can resist; they do have some voice in their own fate.

To counter in the minds of his readers the false ideals instilled by the man-of-war world, Melville in *White-Jacket* repeatedly exposes as butchery the so-called glory of war—the very opposite of old Ushant's kind of glory. White-Jacket feels that were the secret history of all sea heroes written, their laurels would turn to ashes on their brows. "And thinking of all the cruel carnal glory wrought out by naval heroes . . . I asked myself whether, indeed, that was a glorious coffin in which Lord Nelson was entombed," (lxxiv, 316). Desire for glory is condemned in the chapter in which rumors of war reach the *Neversink* when, in contrast to the common sailors, the officers on the quarterdeck welcome the thought of hostilities.

> But why this contrast between the forecastle and the quarter-deck, between the man-of-war's man and his officer? Because, though war would equally jeopardize the lives of both, yet, while it held out to the sailor no promise of promotion, and what is called *glory,* these things fired the breast of his officers.
>
> It is no pleasing task, nor a thankful one, to dive into the souls of some men; but there are occasions when, to bring up the mud from the bottom, reveals to us on what soundings we are, on what coast we adjoin.
>
> How were these officers to gain glory? How but by a distinguished slaughtering of their fellow-men. How were they to be promoted? How but over the buried heads of killed comrades and mess-mates. (xlix, 208)

The truth beneath the lies of "glory"—the reality Melville calls "the glory of the shambles" (lxxiv, 314)—is made to live for the reader as for White-Jacket when Tawney, the elderly black sheet-anchor man, who is one of the best and most intelligent men on the ship—a "truth-telling" man—gives the details of the *Neversink*'s battle, during the War of 1812, with the British ship *Macedonian* (311–16), in which the American ship was victorious, possibly because of superiority in arms, possibly because the impressed English seamen on the *Macedonian,* filled with a spirit of hatred to the service and of a war into which they had been dragged from the arms of their wives, may have spiked her guns. As Tawney and White-Jacket walk together, Tawney points out ineffaceable indentations on the main-deck batteries. Although these have been coated over with the accumulated paint of thirty years, and the scars are not noticeable to the casual eye, Tawney knows them by heart; for he was one of the *Macedonian*'s impressed American merchant seamen who, after the battle, returned on the *Neversink:* "This part of the ship we called the *slaughter-house* on board the Macedonian. Here the men fell, five and six at a time. . . . The beams and carlines overhead in the Macedonian *slaughter-house* were spattered with blood and brains. About the hatchways it looked like a butcher's stall; bits of human flesh sticking in the ring-bolts." And Melville, through Tawney, places the wounded "between the guns."

Melville's desire to show the reality of war beneath the glorifying "paint" motivates also Chapter xvi, "General Training in a Man-of-war." Here, after describing a mock battle during training, White-Jacket tries to imagine what a real battle would be like, the young sailor knowing—like Melville—that "there is always a vast difference—if you sound them—between a reality and a sham." He imagines hospital cots dragged forth on deck and amputation tables "whereon to carve the bodies of the maimed." How different would be this aftermath of a real battle from the orderly appearance on deck and the return to routine duties following the mock battle; how different from the end of the training day is the end of the day of the battle in White-Jacket's imagination! Note the name "Jack Jewel," an early expression of Melville's idea—most fully developed in *Billy Budd*—that war kills the jewel of mankind.

> *Then,* upon mustering the men, and calling the quarter-bills by the light of a battle-lantern, many a wounded seaman, with his arm in a sling, would answer for some poor shipmate who could never more make answer for himself:
> "Tom Brown?"
> "Killed, sir."
> "Jack Jewel?"

"Killed, sir."
"Joe Hardy?"
"Killed, sir."   (69–70)

Again, war and murder are synonymous: the men's names are
written down on the quarter-bills in red ink, "a murderer's fluid,
fitly used on these occasions."

What god do the foremost states of Christendom really worship?
"The God of War," White-Jacket's polemics and Melville's conceptual imagery reply. The contrast between the religion of peace
that Christianity is supposed to be and the actual religion its ad-
herents practice is continually in Melville's mind. The whole matter of war smites Christianity in the face and savors of the devil,
says White-Jacket (lxxiv, 315). Anticipating Melville's conception
of Queequeg in *Moby-Dick,* the sailor asks: "Are there no Mora-
vians in the Moon, that not a missionary has yet visited this poor
pagan planet of ours, to civilize civilization and to christianize
Christendom?" (lxiv, 267). He thinks of officers on a man of war as
"priests of Mars" (xlix, 209). There is the irony he sees when, as the
Neversink leaves Rio, the mainmast of a fighting frigate in its wake
terminates "like a steepled cathedral, in the bannered cross of the
religion of peace" (lxv, 268)—the germ of the poetic concept of the
Bellipotent as a cathedral of the religion of war, developed in *Billy
Budd.* The fiercest possible accusation against any Christian chaplain—that he acts as Judas did—comes in the last of a series of
questions, the first of which is: "How can it be expected that the
religion of peace should flourish in an oaken castle of war?"

> How is it to be expected that when, according to XLII of the
> Articles of War, as they now stand unrepealed on the Statute
> Book, "a bounty shall be paid" (to the officers and crew) "by
> the United States government of $20 for each person on board
> any ship of an enemy which shall be sunk or destroyed by any
> United States ship;" and when, by a subsequent section (vii.),
> it is provided, among other apportionings, that the chaplain
> shall receive "two twentieths" of this price paid for sinking
> and destroying ships full of human beings? How is it to be
> expected that a clergyman, thus provided for, should prove

efficacious in enlarging upon the criminality of Judas, who, for thirty pieces of silver, betrayed his Master? (xxxviii, 157).

The *Neversink's* chaplain never speaks up against the vices of the nineteenth-century world, eminently illustrated by "fighting, flogging, and oppression" (156), in contrast to White-Jacket, to whom each person is the "image of his Creator." (It is reasonable to believe that Melville gives his narrator the thoughts a Christian is supposed to have, not, as Lawrance Thompson thinks, to satirize the sailor's ideals,[21] but precisely for the purpose of spotlighting contrasts between the ideals and the actualities. Melville's quarrel in *White-Jacket* is with the ways of the "foremost states of Christendom," not with their professed religion, most of whose supposed social beliefs he shares.) The picture of a man-of-war's chaplain delivering his sermon to a crew led to the spot by "Go to prayers, d——n you" is one of the outstanding canvases in *White-Jacket* (155–57). In it there is a significant change from what Melville would have observed on the *United States,* whose "Ship's Scribe" describes its chaplain delivering his sermon while standing at "the Desk," [22] whereas in the *White-Jacket* scene one finds, "Fancy, now, this transcendental divine standing behind a gun-carriage." A gun carriage is the mount for a large gun; the chaplain's sermon is the antithesis of the Sermon on the Mount. With this change Melville transforms what would have been a simple documentary report into a symbolic picture that conveys in one glimpse the role played by a Christian chaplain serving "in an oaken castle of war." The canvas could be entitled, as another chapter is, "Prayers at the Guns" (lxix). In the chapter that immediately follows, "Monthly Muster round the Capstan" (lxx), the Sermon on the Mount is openly contrasted with the Articles of War that must be for White-Jacket, as for any common sailor, "the law and gospel . . . whereby I lived, and moved, and had my being" (292–93). Thus, with Paul's quotation from the poet, that is, with reference to yet another Christian text, Melville again places in opposition the pretended religion and the actual religion of the man-of-war world.

The *Neversink's* real God being War, life on it is inevitably hostile to all good and amicable to all evil. Everything in the documentary-poetic portion of the book develops or illustrates this idea, with narration and exposition moving back and forth between the antigood and proevil manifestations and influences.

One set of distributed chapters supports White-Jacket's general statement near the end that the Articles of War create a "system of cruel cogs and wheels, systematically grinding up in one common hopper all that might minister to the moral well-being of the crew" (lxxxix, 374–75). These chapters show the best human qualities of a man-of-war's men to be corrupted by the oppressive, war-directed environment in which the sailors' lives are spent: the gunner's gang growl and curse "as if all their consciences had been powder-singed, and made callous, by their calling"; and a topman, once a merry, companionable fellow, charges at his former friends with his rammer when he is promoted to a quarter gunner's berth, the change in him "solely brought about by his consorting with those villainous, irritable, ill-tempered cannon" (xii, 44–45). Sailors given double their allowance of drink on the Fourth of July fight out "between the guns" the hate largely engendered and fed by the purpose and conditions of man-of-war life. A young boy, flogged for the first time, warns, "Let them look out for me now!" (xxxiii, 138). Similarly, White-Jacket, about to be flogged, is driven to thoughts of murder and suicide. The symbolic meaning of another chapter, "A Man-of-war Button divides two Brothers" (lix), is that the forms of the man-of-war world destroy families and "brotherhood." English-born Jack Chase, ordinarily a man of feeling and not a "national chauvinist," tells with enthusiasm in "Sink, Burn, and Destroy" (lxxv) how the Battle of Navarino, in which he took part, was won, and White-Jacket concludes that on the day of that battle Jack's God was the British Commodore in the Levant and that war makes blasphemers of the best of men: "Some man-of-war's-men have confessed to me, that as a battle has raged more and more, their hearts have hardened in infernal harmony; and, like their own guns, they have fought without a thought" (320). Officers, as a class, do not like a seaman who has "traits of moral sensitiveness, whose demeanor shows some dignity within"; they find him a continual reproach to themselves: "He is unendurable, as an erect, lofty-minded African would be to some slave-driving planter" (xc, 385); indeed, Captain Claret's reaction to old Ushant's defense of his human rights illustrates the enmity of the man-of-war world to whatever is best in "the People."

The *Neversink*, whose very object is destruction, assaults whatever is creative in humankind. The story of Lemsford's poetry, blown up by the gun in which he has hidden it for protection, is entertainingly told, but it is not merely an amusing anecdote. Lemsford, called a "jewel" by Jack Chase, as Billy Budd is by the captain of the *Rights-of-Man,* is a sailor whose spirit White-Jacket finds akin to his own. He is a man "so thoroughly inspired with the divine afflatus, that not even all the tar and tumult of a man-of-war could drive it out of him" (xi, 40). His story is told to show the fate of creative art in a man-of-war world. Another sailor writes and illustrates a journal critical of naval abuses, and the men, to whom he reads it "between the guns," find it a miracle of art and collaborate by collecting material for him. The journal is seized by the master-at-arms; a large nail is driven through it (in a kind of crucifixion); and after that, it is, like an executed sailor, thrown overboard. Music, too, is driven out of the *Neversink:* an immemorial rule forbids sailors on a man of war to sing out at their tasks. Human talents and craftsmanship are wasted in war and in training for war; such is the large implied meaning of Chapter xviii, "A Man-of-war Full as a Nut," in which White-Jacket asserts: "Wrecked on a desert shore, a man-of-war's crew could quickly found an Alexandria by themselves, and fill it with all the things which go to make up a capital." It is a fact "that many good handicraftsmen are lost to their trades and the world by serving in men-of-war" (74).

A complementary set of chapters shows not only how good is assaulted but how the potential for evil in men is fed in a man-of-war world. This is especially true of those in power. Captain Claret is not condemned as vicious in and of himself: "let it not be supposed that it is here sought to impale him before the world as a cruel, black-hearted man. Such he was not. . . . In a word, of whatever acts Captain Claret might have been guilty in the Neversink, perhaps none of them proceeded from any personal, organic hard-heartedness. What he was, the usages of the Navy had made him" (lxxxvii, 367). Of the British officers so hungry for glory and full pay that they were cheered by the possibility of the renewal of the Napoleonic wars, White-Jacket says, "I urge it not against them as *men*—their feelings belonged to their profession. Had they not been naval officers, they had not been rejoicers in the midst of despair" (xlix, 209). Even the villainous Bland, the master-at-arms, is one whose evil goes with his function. Telling of him in "A Knave in Office in a Man-of-war" (xliv), White-Jacket states that he will not take the Day of Judgment upon himself by pronouncing upon the essential evil of any man-of-war's man (188). To be sure, it seems contradictory that White-Jacket should at the same time speak of Bland as an "organic scoundrel." But it should come through to the reader—with the help of the echoed word *organic*— that Bland is, on the symbolic level, the embodiment of the evil "absolutely organic to a Navy establishment." His poetic role, that of *Billy Budd*'s Claggart in embryo, is communicated first by Melville's description of him. Like Claggart, Bland suggests the Devil, with which image Melville again and again associates war. His "fine polish" is the equivalent of the paint over the battle scars on the *Neversink* and of its spit-and-polish appearance. So he is a personification of the "glazed-over" evil of war. Looking and conversing in a "gentlemanly" manner, he exerts his civilization's brute Force: he "officially" seizes men to be flogged and plays a "conspicuous" part in the scourgings. Moreover, his story echoes what is implied by his description. The captain favors him, welcoming both his presents and his zeal in the performance of his function. He is unimaginable in any habitat other than the man-of-war world that has chosen him for the position of master-at-arms it has itself created. His power to do the men harm resides *only* in this position; during his period of suspension he is "like a disarmed sword-fish." The captain, needing his services, publicly reinstates him "in his office" after his brief time out of it. Finally, pointing up Bland's role as the incarnation of the evil essential, in both meanings of that word, to the war machine, Melville lets the reader know that after the voyage ends, the navy rehires him "in his old capacity." Bland's organic evil, then, is "organic" in the etymological sense, "like an organ, tool, instrument," and in the military sense, "assigned to and constituting a permanent part of a military organization under its table of organization and equipment." [23]

Not only is good assaulted and evil fostered in a man-of-war world, but what in another environment might be a great good is, in the service of war, turned into a gross evil. In particular, institutions and professions originally intended to protect life menace it instead. Such an ironic reality can be communicated only by indirection. In the work as a whole this reality is implied about the American navy as, by extension, to all standing armies and navies. It is signified by the leaky lifebuoys that sink the men who cling to them and by the hammocks, elsewhere perfect for sleep, that in the navy become "Bastilles." Above all, this idea is developed in the four-chapter Cuticle story, a great work of fiction in itself.

Extraordinary in its coruscating effect of glittering satire combined with dark drama, this section (lx–lxiii, 246–64), is the single most effective reinforcement of the idea that the man-of-war world is the antithesis of what the world should be. It creates a microcosm of the *Neversink* world, concentrating in one intensely visual scene the threefold choice that the book as a whole presents: life or death; acquiescence or dissent; the values of war or of peace. It reveals, by means of grotesque art, the misuse of most knowledge in the man-of-war world. The field of medicine provides Melville with his grotesque, unforgettable demonstration of the distortion of the role of knowledge.

A foretopman denied liberty goes overboard in the Bay of Rio hoping he will be able to lower a canoe and paddle himself ashore. He is shot at by the sentry. A musket bullet enters his thigh just above the knee, and he is taken back on board. The medical question, whether or not to amputate, is considered. No other methods are tried in the meantime, and his condition worsens. Cuticle (dead skin), Surgeon of the Fleet, who is stationed on the *Neversink* and who is reported to be the foremost surgeon in the navy (no mere exception, but outstanding representative), has full authority to decide. He is the book's example, par excellence, of the metamorphosis of man into function. Even physically he is hardly a person but rather a collection of fabricated parts: "He walked abroad, a curious patch-work of life and death, with a wig, one glass eye, and a set of false teeth." From the moment the sailor is taken on board, Cuticle is enthusiastically determined to amputate, but before he does, he invites the surgeons of the neighboring American ships of war to attend what Melville calls a "ceremonious consultation." None of his colleagues is convinced of the need to operate, but when Surgeon Cuticle proceeds as if they agree, no one protests. The operation is performed in a screened-off place. Again Melville brings in the mechanism on which the large guns are mounted: "Upon two gun-carriages, dragged amidships, the Death-board (used for burials at sea) was horizontally placed." From the long horizontal pole of a gun rammer hang towels with "U.S." marked on them, the monogram a reminder to the reader that the U.S. Navy is not a thing in itself but the armed force of a foremost state of Christendom. Melville says one thing through Cuticle, who intends another. Lecturing to the younger medical men before demonstrating his skill, the surgeon bemoans the dull time of peace and advises his juniors that if the war then threatening between the United States and Mexico should break out, they should exchange their navy commissions for commissions in the army: "The army, young gentlemen, is your best school; depend upon it." Then he snatches off his wig, takes out his set of false teeth, spirits his glass eye out of his head with professional dexterity, and "divested of nearly all inorganic appurtenances, what was left of the Surgeon slightly shook itself," readying itself for the operation—an impersonal thing signifying what remains in the navy of the original conception of what a doctor should be. The topman, stretched upon the table, surrounded by glittering knives and saws, towels and sponges, is an image of helplessness in the face of arbitrary power, and the reader is confronted with the contrast between life and needless death as the surgeon (in Melville's mind, turned carpenter) proceeds to operate. (The passage contains a reminder that the sailor was the victim, in the first place, of a gun.)

Now the Surgeon of the Fleet and the top-man presented a spectacle which, to a reflecting mind, was better than a church-yard sermon on the mortality of man.

Here was a sailor, who, four days previous, had stood erect—a pillar of life—with an arm like a royal-mast and a thigh like a windlass. But the slightest conceivable finger-touch of a bit of crooked trigger had eventuated in stretching him out, more helpless than an hour-old babe, with a blasted thigh, utterly drained of its brawn. And who was it that now stood over him like a superior being, and, as if clothed himself with the attributes of immortality, indifferently discoursed of carving up his broken flesh, and thus piecing out his abbreviated days? Who was it, that in capacity of Surgeon, seemed enacting the part of a Regenerator of life? The withered, shrunken, one-eyed, toothless, hairless Cuticle; with a trunk half dead—a *memento mori* to behold!

Although the bullet entered near the sailor's knee, Surgeon Cuticle cuts near the point of articulation with the trunk: "Now, young gentlemen, you can not but perceive, that the point of operation being so near the trunk and the vitals, it becomes an unusually beautiful one, demanding a steady hand and a true eye." A surgeon's assistant at the foot of the operating table waits in readiness to receive the limb, "as when a plank is being severed by a carpenter and his apprentice." Then Life and the attack on it are again symbolized: "Not a breath was heard; but as the quivering flesh parted in a long, lingering gash, a spring of blood welled up between the living walls of the wound, and two thick streams, in opposite driections, coursed down from the thigh," a picture suggesting, with what follows, the rivers of blood shed and the Life casually wasted in a world of war. The following evening the former messmates of the topman row his remains ashore and bury them in the "ever-vernal" Protestant cemetery in plain sight of the bay, where the Judgment Day of the whole world's men of war is to take place. The story of how the topman is first shot and then finished off on the operating table uncovers the reality—as grim as the skeleton the surgeon dangles in front of his victims as he is about to make his cut—of the fate carved out for the common man in a man-of-war world. Yet Cuticle, too, is a product of that world; once, presumably, he was not an old, hairless, toothless, one-eyed remnant of a man. As with Bland, it is the navy that gives him his power over the men. What is more, it is the navy that sets up the apparatus of "consultation" and training by means of which the Surgeon of the Fleet cuts new young surgeons to the same established pattern to which he has been fashioned.

The last three chapters of *White-Jacket* (Ch. xcii, "The last of the Jacket"; Ch. xciii, "Cable and Anchor all clear; and "The End") are a poetic summary of what the work as a whole has had to say about the "whole present social frame-work of our world" (lxxvi, 324). The narration that includes White-Jacket's descent into the underworld of the sea, his vision of the end of war, and his view of the man of war as microcosm of the contemporary world is a distillation of the understandings the young sailor has brought out of the hell of the *Neversink*. Returned to life by his own choice and struggle, and aided by the crew, White-Jacket looks back on his experience and declares his faith in a "God" of peace and brotherhood, implied to be latent in each of us, though there is no assurance that what is latent will awaken. White-Jacket's symbolic choice between life and death is still to be made by the "People"; many, he tells us, though they say they will not, sign up again on men of war. White-Jacket's last appeal is, "[L]et us never train our murderous guns inboard; let us not mutiny with bloody pikes in our hands" (398). Since everything in "The End" is figurative, and the *Neversink* is no longer a ship or a country but "this earth that sails through the air," *mutiny* is neither literal nor limited in meaning. It is the mutiny against Life and humanity that is war: let us never train our guns against our fellow human beings is the implication.

White-Jacket, whose inclusive theme is predicted by the passages from *Mardi* and *Omoo* cited at the beginning of this intepretation, itself predicts works of Melville to come. Its final image of all Earth as a man of war brings Melville's imagination to the threshold of *Moby-Dick* in which another ship, resembling a man of war in its prime purpose and in its enslavement of the crew to that purpose, is symbolic of the supposedly civilized world of Melville's day. Above all, *White-Jacket* points ahead four decades to *Billy Budd*. Two of the many parallel poetic/philosophical concepts of both works are especially relevant here, both of them pointing up Melville's interest in the underlying structure and organization of the man-of-war world. The first parallel may seem shocking, but, like Medusa of whom White-Jacket speaks, it must be viewed. If the "ceremonious consultation" scene in *White-Jacket* is juxtaposed with the drumhead court scene in *Billy Budd,* a terrible similarity of particulars appears—resulting in a similarity of essence—despite the differences. In each scene a sentence is passed, presumably in consultation, but in reality decided by the one who has made his determination on the instant. Neither one considers any alternative to what he wills. Each manipulates the final group acceptance. Melville has each express regret and talk sympathetically to the victim, who is, in *White-Jacket,* a "pillar of life" who was denied "liberty," in *Billy Budd* a jewel of youth and humanity separated from the "Rights of Man." During the operation, Cuticle is a man turned into a knife; at the execution Vere is as if transformed into a musket. It is as if Melville took the same basic reality of the man-of-war world—its needless destruction of life—and placed it in two different kinds of illumination: in the first scene he used the light of harsh satire to condemn that reality; in the second scene he used a less glaring, more penetrating light in order first of all to understand the reality in all its subtleties and contradictions. Though the one scene is grotesque and the other finely shaded, though Cuticle is a caricature whereas Vere is a symbol of civilized man suffering from his dedication to the ways of the man-of-war world, the bare bones of the "present civilization of the world" are identical in the two scenes. The second close poetic parallel in *White-Jacket* and *Billy Budd* is the visual/conceptual one between what White-Jacket imagines might happen to him as an ordinary sailor on a man of war and the final picture of what happens to Billy. Put into the right rhyme and rhythm and substituting "Billy Budd" for "White-Jacket," White-Jacket's thoughts might be a prelude to the ballad of "Billy in the Darbies." The young sailor on the *Neversink* addresses himself in words that the Dansker, if he were a poet, might have spoken to Billy:

> Have a care, then, have a care, lest you come to a sad end, even the end of a rope; lest, with a black-and-blue throat, you turn a dumb diver after pearl shells; put to bed forever, and tucked in, in your own hammock, at the bottom of the sea.

And there you will lie, White-Jacket, while hostile navies are playing cannon-ball billiards over your grave. (lxx, 294)

So long as hostile navies exist, then, common sailors, particularly young ones like White-Jacket or Billy, will be in darbies and continually in danger of needless death.

As, in astronomy, the gravitational pull of the sun must be seen as central if the motions of the planets and their place in the universe are to be understood, so in a study of *White-Jacket* it is necessary to see Melville's hatred of war as the force that explains the place and interrelated motion of all else in the work. *White-Jacket* illustrates outstandingly how central a dynamic in Melville's imagination was his passion against the "greatest of evils" and how strong a pull it exerted in shaping most of his major works from *Mardi* to *Billy Budd*.

Notes

1. Herman Melville, *White-Jacket* (Evanston, Ill.: Northwestern Univ. Press and The Newberry Library, 1970), Ch. xlix, p. 208. All references in the text will be to this edition. In the epigraphs that precede the text, the emphasis on "Jacket" is Melville's; other emphases in the quotations are mine.
2. Herman Melville, *Mardi* (Evanston Northwestern Univ. Press and The Newberry Library, 1970), Ch. clxiv, p. 541.
3. *Moby-Dick*'s phrase "prime purpose" in connection with the *Pequod* seems to me to be an echo of *White-Jacket*'s "very object" in reference to any man of war.
4. Herman Melville, *Omoo* (Evanston, Ill.: Northwestern Univ. Press and The Newberry Library, 1968), Ch. xxix, p. 108n.
5. The usual critical view of *White-Jacket* is that tyranny is the main theme and that condemnation of war, though also important, is secondary.
6. Charles R. Anderson, *Mellville in the South Seas* (New York: Columbia Univ. Press, 1939), and Howard P. Vincent, *The Tailoring of Melville's "White-Jacket"* (Evanston, Ill.: Northwestern Univ. Press, 1970). The patchwork image is Vincent's.
7. I have lifted this phrase from the description of the French warships that appears in the second chapter of *Typee*.
8. White-Jacket's personal story is an "inside narrative" like the "inside narrative" hinted at in the subtitle of *Billy Budd*, that is, the story of a change in consciousness about the world of war, brought about by an experience of its cruelties. In *Billy Budd* the stirring is in the consciousness in the crew and is

expressed for them by the questionings of the sailor-poet. In *White-Jacket*, the young sailor becomes the spokesman for the crew in the book he writes about his experience on the *Neversink*.

9. The generally accepted view is the one developed so fascinatingly by Vincent in *The Tailoring of Melville's "White-Jacket."* This work, a splendid contribution to our knowledge of the sources of *White-Jacket* and of how Melville reworked them, is, in my view, mistaken in its interpretation of the jacket as a psychological and moral symbol of significance only in connection with the narrator as an individual, and hence in its opinion that the two lines of the narrative are disparate pieces awkwardly patched together.

10. Vincent, p. 23.

11. Vincent's use of this phrase (p. 87) reflects his feeling that the white jacket and Redburn's shooting jacket are closely related symbols. But except for the fact that both are jackets, there is no basis in the text for such a connection: Redburn is a boy on his first voyage, awakening painfully to the fact that seafaring is no grand adventure and that he will not suddenly rise to importance in the world; White-Jacket is an experienced sailor with no such illusion, awakening to a more complete, but not astounding, knowledge of the world, in the course of his experience on a man of war. Vincent's concept of the white jacket as a symbol of infancy leads him into several contradictory positions—for example, his speaking near the end (p. 223) of "the placental white-jacket which throughout the novel has been a mockingly destructive agent"—a highly debatable metaphor, in which the placenta has had to be misconceived as a destructive rather than as a nourishing thing.

12. Vincent offers exciting insight into the verbal methods by means of which Melville achieves the sensuous effects in his description of White-Jacket's fall from the yardarm and his sinking into the sea (Chs.17–18).

13. *Mardi*, Ch. lxx, p. 214.

14. My view is that "God" in Melville's art is a poetic image either reflecting the character of the one who conceives that God (as in the case of Ahab) or symbolizing, as in *Battle-Pieces,* Melville's own idea of what is sacred in life.

15. In Chapter 9 of this work other conceptual images common to both works are presented.

16. Herman Melville, *Billy Budd, Sailor (An Inside Narrative),* reading and genetic text edited from the manuscript by Harrison Hayford and Merton M. Sealts, Jr. (Chicago: The Univ. of Chicago Press, 1962), p. 123.

17. *Billy Budd, Sailor,* p. 122.

18. Ibid.

19. *Melville in the South Seas* and *The Tailoring of Melville's "White-Jacket"* abound in passages quoted from the sources Melville used, accompanied by the passages he re-created from those sources.

20. *Mardi*, Ch. cxlii, pp. 453–54.

21. Lawrance Thompson, *Melville's Quarrel with God* (Princeton: Princeton Univ. Press, 1952).

22. Anderson, p. 369.

23. *Webster's Third New International Dictionary.*

4.

Moby-Dick as Symbolic Poem
of War and Peace

Gestation in the poetic imagination is so secret a process that the poet may not even sense that it is going on. Of the five ships on which Melville had worked, from 1839 to 1844, three were whalers, and his voyages on them lasted more than two years.[1] Yet of his first five books, all deriving from his travel experience, not one centers around whaling. *Typee* (1846), *Omoo* (1847), and *Mardi* (1849) begin on whaling vessels, but the narrators soon leave them, as Melville had left those on which he had shipped. And in *Mardi* life on the *Arcturion* is so monotonous, so wearying, the days go so slowly "round and round, endless and uneventful as cycles in space," that centuries seem to pass and the narrator's desire to leave becomes "little short of a frenzy"; he will rail at those "lost and leaden hours" while life lasts:[2] in the context of *Mardi* as a whole, time on the *Arcturion* is an image of eternity. *Redburn* (1849) and *White-Jacket* (1850) do not deal with whaling at all. Then suddenly, not at the start,[3] but in the course of the composition of what would become *Moby-Dick* (1851), as tides began to move back and forth in the work in progress,[4] Melville found that as a whale-man he had been "wrapped by influences all tending to make his fancy pregnant with many a mighty birth."[5] And the "over-whelming idea of the great whale himself" (i, 16) became his "mighty theme" (civ, 379).

55

But while the processes of the poetic imagination take place in inner darkness, they leave traces in the works to which the imagination gives birth. So a theory can be set forth to explain, in a broad, approximate way, how and with what effect it was that the whale, seemingly out of nowhere, should have leaped up when it did in Melville's imagination as the representation of ungraspable life itself, and the world of whaling should have become symbolic of the world to which until then Melville had been responding more directly in his work, though with some considerable degree of symbolism in *Mardi* and *White-Jacket.* The poet's imagination seizes upon a phenomenon as a symbol of an idea only when his or her mind already possesses that idea. Then the objective phenomenon and the preexisting thought mate and, in union, grow. By 1850 Melville had explored all his travel experiences whose meanings were intrinsic (as distinguished from connotative)—from his observation of the "civilized" war on "savage" peace that the colonialists and their accessories were waging in the Pacific to his observation of life and the destruction of life aboard the battleship *United States.* Once his initial probing of these experiences had been completed, once his ever growing view of the "civilized" and "Christian" world as a world of war had climaxed, at the end of *White-Jacket,* in his vision of Earth as a man of war on which the Articles of War form the "domineering code," the whaling ship could, almost as a natural next visualization, appear to him as like a man of war (and hence also as symbolic of the world), and the whale could become the symbol of Life at which makers of war, in essence, strike. Conversely, once the world view that Melville had already developed united with the poetic conception that the whaling world could represent it, the war-or-peace theme of his earlier works became transformed, not only finding symbolic expression, but also expanding into an all-encompassing philosophy of life. From the union within his "outreaching" imagination of his whaling experience and his world view, a work evolved in which the spirit of war, as embodied in Life-hating Ahab, and the spirit of peace, as symbolized by Life-preserving Queequeg, represent the fundamental impulses in the human heart, which had been and remained at the center of Melville's universe. *Moby-Dick* became something new in literature (in which works about war had always

been set in the theater of, or against the background of, war between opposing groups of men); it became a symbolic poem about
the "soul" of war and the "soul" of peace.

But *Moby-Dick* is a symbolic poem that is also intensely realistic,
with the immediacy and convincingness that symbolic expression
often lacks. For it to have this duality, something else unique in
fiction had to come into existence—a "complementarity" of vision
analogous to that of modern physics that finds a combination of
"contradictory" ways of looking at certain things (outstandingly,
light as both waves and corpuscles) necessary to a more complete
understanding of what is under consideration. What Melville was
trying to achieve in *Moby-Dick* was a fuller and deeper understanding than he had reached in *Mardi* of the essence of the world of his
day and, at the same time, the relation of that world to all of time
and space. He recognized that it is impossible "attentively, and
completely, to examine any two things" at once, that if the human
mind is brought to bear on one thing, "the other will be utterly
excluded from . . . contemporary consciousness" (lxxiv, 279–80). So
he created a way of looking, on the one hand, at the actualities of
whaling, hinting at what they might suggest about the world, and,
on the other hand, at those aspects of Leviathan that made him
think of "the whole circle of the sciences, and all the generations of
whales, and men, and mastodons, past, present, and to come, with
all the revolving panoramas of empire on earth, and throughout
the whole universe, not excluding its suburbs" (civ, 379). With
these complementary ways of looking, it was possible to consider in
alternation, and then to suggest in mental interrelation, all the
realities hinted at, and united by, the whale: the transitory and
the continuing; the immediate and the remote; the concrete and
the abstract; outer world and inner; individual and species; one
life and Life. The world of Melville's day, as it is made visible in
the drama of Ahab, the crew, the ship, and the whale, against the
infinite background of sea merging into sky, is viewed at times in
detail, as under a microscope, and at other times in context, as part
of the endless, seamless fabric of all existence.

The drama can be recalled in twenty-odd lines, so elementary
are the principles with which it deals. In the whaling village of
New Bedford, a bitter youth, Ishmael, the narrator, is partly (and

prophetically) redeemed from his hatred of the world and life by Queequeg, a "pagan" harpooner with whom he has been thrown together and who becomes his bosom friend. Queequeg has come from a remote island to study the ways of the Christians, but he cannot yet return for he feels that life among Christians has corrupted him and he must first be purified. Against the advice of an old sailor-prophet Elijah, Ishmael and Queequeg take employment on the whaler *Pequod,* becoming members of a crew that is to be conscripted in Captain Ahab's private war against Moby Dick. This great white whale had taken off Ahab's leg, when on an earlier voyage he had assaulted it, and it had thus provided him with a visible and assailable object on which to vent his hatred of life. Since no member of the crew truly opposes Ahab, he takes down with him in the battle with Moby Dick all the races of mankind represented by the crew and all the "values" represented by the ship. Only Ishmael survives, saved by Queequeg's canoe-coffin acting as a lifebuoy, on whose lid are markings copied there from inscriptions long ago tattooed on his body in the place of his origin. For a day and a night Ishmael floats as if alone in the universe. Then he is picked up by the *Rachel* whose lifesaving mission is the opposite of the one that had been the *Pequod*'s.

That the main theme of this drama is whether man will continue to be directed to destruction by the "death-dealing" spirit of war or will be saved by the spirit of life-preserving brotherhood is sustained, first, by the fundamental war-and-peace imagery in which Melville brings the narrative to life and in the associations and correspondences he sees: Ahab and Queequeg are part of this overall imagery.

War imagery characterizes not only the scenes of battle with the whale but all portrayals of ship and crew; of roles and relationships; of goals, machinery, and methods. Melville does not intend the reader to forget—not even in the most realistic chapters on the dissection of the whale or in chapters that seem to be digressions—that the "prime but private purpose" (xlvi, 184) of the *Pequod*'s voyage is Ahab's war.

The *Pequod* (like the other quintessential warship of Melville in "The Haglets") is a "thing of trophies." Like the battleship *Neversink* in *White-Jacket,* it is ultimately bound for its own destruction.

Melville chooses as its name the Algonquin word for destroyer. It gores the white waves in its "madness." [6] Ahab, its captain, is regularly and exclusively associated with conquerors and martial commanders—for example, Xerxes, Alexander, and Tamerlane. He stands like a fencer at one end of his boat; his glance shoots "like a javelin with the pointed intensity of his purpose." His mates are "as captains of companies," and the men about to throw themselves into the whaleboat look like "the long line of man-of-war's men about to throw themselves on board an enemy's ship." A new sailor in his first encounter with the whale resembles a raw army recruit "marching from the bosom of his wife into the fever heat of his first battle." [7]

Reminders of war appear in almost every connection. Thoughts of whaling pictures by the painter Garneray remind Ishmael of battle pictures lining the gallery of the triumphal hall at Versailles. The weight of the ocean on the whale's back is estimated in terms of the weight of twenty line-of-battle ships with all their guns and stores and men on board. The shadows that the three whaleboats send down could shade half of Xerxes' army. A waif pole stuck in a killed whale to mark him as the property of a ship that must temporarily go off is like a nation's flag on newly taken territory.

The whales, swimming together, are a "grand armada"; they arc met in vast herds, "as if numerous nations of them had sworn solemn league and covenant for mutual assistance and protection." The multitude hurries through the straits in the same way as "marching armies approaching an unfriendly defile in the mountains, accelerate their march, all eagerness to place that perilous passage in their rear." When they sense that the boats are after them, they form "in close ranks and battalions," so that their spouts look "like flashing lines of stacked bayonets" (lxxxvii, 318–22).

All the encounters with the whales, before the one with Moby Dick, are like battle scenes, but they are whaling scenes as well. The final battle with Moby Dick (cxxxv, 463–69), the climax toward which Melville, like Ahab, has been driving from the beginning, is not only like war, it *is* war, and nothing else but war. Melville announces that this scene should be so viewed when he has sharks follow Ahab's whaleboat in the same way that "vultures hover over the banners of marching regiments in the east." Now no purpose but Ahab's war on Life exists. His "slogan" tears every other cry but his to shreds. His body is pure weapon, his emotion pure hate, as, somewhat like a crossbow or catapult "with body arched back, and both arms high-lifted to the poise, he darted his fierce iron, and his far fiercer curse into the hated whale." The last view of him, caught round the neck and pulled out of the boat by the line, after his harpoon has been thrown, presents visually Melville's belief that warmaking purposes lead on to self-destruction. The final view of the *Pequod* gives pictorial expression to the same idea on the largest possible scale, as the ship, which has been to Melville like the "man-of-war world" of his age, goes down. The last thing seen is the flag Ahab has ordered hammered back on the mainmast; wrapped in it is a skyhawk, "a living part of heaven," caught between the hammer (which thus, too, becomes a weapon) and the yet visible sinking top inches of the spar.

The effect of the war imagery is intensified by the contrasting imagery of peace that alternates with it in the oceanic rhythm of the work. Bloody scenes follow or precede such scenes of serenity as that of the "sea pastures" of the Pacific, the "heart" of the earth, whose wide-rolling watery prairies, once beheld by any "meditative Magian rover" (Melville), must ever after be the sea of his choice. An effective contrast in this scene shows Ahab watching the serene sea and anticipating the shedding of Moby Dick's blood; his firm lips, met like the lips of a vise, show that his choice is for what is warlike, not pacific (cxi, 399–400). The final battle is preceded by a scene of peace in which Ahab lifts his "helmet" of a brow to the azure feminine air. But although he drops a tear into the sea, he still turns his back on peace and "all natural lovings." The last battle is followed by a final scene purged of war. The destruction caused by Ahab has been drawn down into the sea, which rolls on "as it rolled five thousand years ago," a reminder of the biblical flood that God sent because "the earth was filled with violence."

An abstract idea of woman is an essential part of the peace imagery, as in the reference, just cited, to the feminine air. She represents those desirable things in life for which there is no place in war. The descriptions of nature at peace bear this out. So does the fact that the ship involved in the search to save life is the one with a woman's name, that of Rachel who wept for her children slain by Herod. The banishment of the feminine from the lives of the men on the *Pequod* is highlighted in the scene in the forecastle at midnight, which ends in a fight. In the case of Ahab, the absence of Woman in his life is especially stressed: his "sweet mother" was unknown to him, and he left for Cape Horn the day after his marriage, which took place when he was past fifty. In the embattled herd of whales, there is a feminine haven of peace: in the innermost part of the herd, as if the core of continuing life is being protected there, are "the women and children" of the host, and below the transparent surface float the nursing mothers and those soon to be mothers. "And thus, though surrounded by circle upon circle of consternations and affrights, did these inscrutable creatures at the centre freely and fearlessly indulge in all peaceful concernments." Even the whalemen in the boat with Ishmael, interrupted in their battle because they are hemmed in, are entranced, and he, relating the scene (lxxxvii–viii, 324–30), thinks of the peaceful place "deep down and deep inland" that is in him and, by implication, in man. To confirm the impression of the feminine as representative of peace, community, and the original latent good in the heart of man, Melville ends the section with a contrast between the males of the herd who desert a wounded comrade and the females who always try to save a companion even at the risk of death. But the feminine nature of so much of the peace imagery does not mean that *Moby-Dick* expresses the untenable idea that in the human race the female half is by nature peaceful and the male half inherently warlike. The main human symbol of peace and community in the book is Queequeg, whose lifesaving aims are regularly counterposed to the antilife purpose of Ahab that is expressed in his war on Moby Dick.

For all-inclusive, endless, evanescent, never all-knowable life is what Moby Dick, the consummate instance of his species, incarnates. He is not in Melville's imagination what he is in Ahab's—the "horror" of life and nature alone. But many have thought him so, and since the whale's significance, both in his "broad genera" and in his quintessence as Moby Dick, is at the heart of the book (one-fourth of which is made up of chapters exclusively about the whale), the interpretation of Leviathan as Melville's symbol of life in its most comprehensive sense must be firmly established. Ahab's meaning and stature in the total conception depend on the meaning and scope of the whale. Everything from the full title, *Moby-Dick; or, The Whale,* to the last view of Moby Dick disappearing into the sea after the great battle, shows the whale to be the key conceptual image.

A one-page "Etymology" and ten pages of "Extracts" precede the narrative and constitute a two-part prelude that hints at the meaning to Melville of this central image. The "Etymology" lists the word for whale in thirteen languages, including Fegee, Icelandic, Hebrew, Greek, Latin, and Anglo-Saxon, thus immediately suggesting the universality of the whale and the fact that he has long existed. The extracts, quotations from what has been said of Leviathan by people of many nations and generations, express principally the awe that is felt worldwide at the whale's immensity and at the vast current of life that courses within him.

The narrative itself reverberates with correspondences between the whale, particularly the sperm whale, and life. Indomitable, embodying energy on the most prodigious scale, he is designated throughout by epithets intended to convey him as the largest warm-blooded figure of life. He is the "king of creation," the "largest inhabitant of the globe," a "mass of tremendous life," the creature with "a surplus stock of vitality in him," able to exist for a long time under water as well as in the air. He is "immortal in his species, however perishable in his individuality." In him "you feel the Deity and the dread powers more forcibly than in beholding any other object in living nature." That he symbolizes life in its entirety on earth is implied by the imaginative association of the slowly revolving dying whale with a "waning world" and of the whale's death at sunset with the "death" of the sun. The male whale's huge penis, the female whale's sex characteristics, the seminal and life-continuing connotations of the word *sperm* all convey the idea of vast procreative and life-sustaining powers. The writer who gropes down into the bottom of the sea after the whale has his hands "among the . . . foundations, ribs, and very pelvis of the world." Even the "funeral" of a whale lights by contrast the vitality of the living whale; even the description of the squid, which the crew mistakes for Moby Dick, carries the idea of the whale as life; the squid is only "an unearthly, formless, chance-like *apparition of life*" (my emphasis).[8]

In the whale, as in life, all time is united. He comes down to us from the "headwaters of the Eternities." He "swam the seas before the continents broke water." What of his future? Can he long endure "so wide a chase, and so remorseless a havoc"? Can he outlast the "everlasting war" on him? Yes. As he is "the mightiest animated mass that has survived the flood," so if there is another flood, "the eternal whale will still survive." As he has outlived previous civilizations, so at the end of the narrative he outlives the one whose spirit has been breathed into Ahab and which the *Pequod* symbolizes: the last chapter relates that Moby Dick, though Ahab's harpoon had struck him, "flew forward"; and in the "Epilogue," life from the *Pequod* does fly forward in Ishmael.

The whale, like life, unites all places. Moby Dick seems "ubiquitous," being spotted in far-flung places almost simultaneously, so swiftly does he travel. The whale of old left his wake along the present lines of the Andes and the Himalayas. Cetus, the whale constellation, unites earth and sky. He seems to have swum from the sea into the heavens, for Melville, like Queequeg, sees the oceans of earth and those of space as one interflowing sea.

At the same time that he unites environments and times, Melville's whale unites different states of being. The description of a whale's skeleton on a tropical island joins sea and land; sun and earth; animal, plant, and human; life and death; time past, present, and to come. The skeleton was found with its head against a coconut tree whose "plumage-like tufted droopings" seemed the whale's "verdant jet." Then the skeleton was moved to a glen to be both god and chapel in a temple of palm trees. Strange hieroglyphics were carved on the vertebrae to record the life of the islanders. A flame kept burning in the skull sends forth a vapory spout. The vines that grow around it suggest to Ishmael life enfolding death, death trellising life. He sees the sun shining down through the palm fronds, and, making a design of light and shade, weaving a "freshet-rushing carpet that forever slides away," in the one image suggesting both the evanescence and the continuity of life.

Finally the whale, like life, includes the finite known and infinite unknown. It suggests all that we at any time do not know and can only imagine, life being infinitely more vast and swiftly changing than the combined knowledge of men of any time. For Melville knew, as does present-day science, though the science of his day generally did not, that since life is always on the move, if we try to stop it to analyze it, its living reality escapes us. He sees the whale, like life again, defying systematic classification and characterization: as yet the sperm whale, "scientific or poetic, lives not complete in any literature." The whale's movements cannot be predicted; his shape keeps changing. "Dissect him how I may . . . I but go skin deep; I know him not, and never will." Like books, pictures of the whale (read also other artistic or religious interpretations of life), whether Egyptian, Hindu, Christian, or "Hogarthian," can never show him fully as he is. Most of his life is submerged in unfathomable waters, and where he obtains his sustenance is unknown. The source of his life (like the source of Life) is mysterious: when an individual whale is fatally wounded, and the red tide of blood (which in Deuteronomy 12:23 is "the life") flows out of him, "his life may be said to pour from him in incessant streams" like a river "whose source is in the well-springs of far-off and indiscernible hills." Beneath his body's thin glassy outer covering are markings like mystic hieroglyphics on ancient rocks. And always the broad "firmament" of his forehead is pleated with riddles, which it depends on one's mood, Melville says, or on one's character or quality of mind, the narrative implies, to interpret in one way or another. The whale is a test of the imagination, as is the doubloon in the story. As for Ishamel, at times he sees the seeming malice of the whale; at other times he finds him archangelical, sublime.

Such, then, is the whale in general. What of Moby Dick? In essence he does not differ from his species. His distinguishing characteristics serve only to emphasize his whaleness: his uncommon size magnifies it; his whiteness intensifies it. He dramatizes the qualities of his species at the same time that he is, paradoxically, an abstraction of them. He is all-reaching, forward-flowing, enigmatic, self-contradictory life made visible; yet he is also "one grand hooded phantom," by implication the "ungraspable phantom of life" that the echoing word points back to. The chapter devoted to his whiteness finds white the "visible absence of color," but also, since all colors merge in it, "the concrete of all colors." Elusive, complex, subtle, and implying invisible truths, the white whale can, among other things, suggest "all the horrors of the half-known life."

Since the connotations of both *whale* and *white* are so limitless to Melville, is it any wonder that readers have found so many meanings in Moby Dick? He is imaginatively conceived to imply all that there is, or may in the future be, in life.

It is against this image of life, then, that Ahab is at war. In his "narrow-flowing monomania" he sees only one aspect of it—pain and affront to him. He hates it and the "murderer" of a God he imagines created it; yet he would like to be like that God—omniscient, omnipotent, and an inhuman murderer, free of consequences. Though "in his heart" he knows his war to be madness, it is from his heart that Melville has him turn, step by step, until he turns even from the sun that momentarily softens his heart.[9]

In addition to the crescendo of "turnings" from his "humanities," an interweaving of other original methods creates Ahab, the warmaker, for the reader: Melville's extended presentation of him as a deteriorating kind of tragic figure; the images that set forth his character and its devolution; comparisons and contrasts (as during each encounter with another whaling ship); the relationships between him and the crew; the description of the almost total annihilation his war madness causes; and Melville's stress on the fact that Ahab's interpretation of the whale is a matter of his particular Life-hating perception—all lay stress on the way things are continually said to *seem* to him.

The particular kind of tragic figure Melville conceives Ahab to be, and his own view of Ahab's response to life, are revealed by *Moby-Dick*'s full, sustained parallel with *Macbeth.* Phrases and concepts from Shakespeare's drama flash at regular intervals throughout the narrative, and the conception of "fair" and "foul" keeps recurring up to the moment when the line runs "foul," catching Ahab around the neck despite the seemingly fair prophecies of Fedallah. Characters in both dramas play roles almost identical in purpose. Macbeth wants to be king of Scotland; Ahab wants to be king of all. Both set aside reason and their humanities, one by one, and plunge their worlds into war. Both shift responsibility to Fate. Melville consciously transforms the witches into Fedallah: the deceptions of Macbeth by the witches and of Ahab by Fedallah are all self-deceptions; the archfiend that leads each one on to killing resides in himself. Both want to think they can bear a charmed life free of the laws of cause and effect. Knowing his end to be near, each rails at his subordinates to vent his fury at reality. Neither is the kind of tragic hero who achieves profound self-understanding or illumination of life; each arrives at only a spitting defiance, Melville almost spelling this out in Ahab's last speech: "I spit my last breath at thee." Ultimately each is seen stripped of his last human ties, bonded instead to his weapon, striking at life and cursing it. In the end Macbeth, too, rejects even the sun—he begins to be aweary of it—and wishes "the estate o' the world were now undone." Yet in part of his split mind each protagonist knows all along that he is self-doomed. Macbeth knows even before the first murder that there is "an even-handed justice" that "commends the ingredients of our poisoned chalice to our own lips." After the first murder he sees at once that the wine of his life is drunk and only the lees are left. Later he laments that he is "in blood steeped in so far" that he cannot turn back to what he once was. He has nothing to spur him on but "vaulting ambition," but that, as he knows, overleaps his reason and human sympathy. In the parallel that Melville meticulously constructs, Ahab instructs the harpooners into whom he pours his spirit(s) to "commend the murderous chalices," only slightly varying Macbeth's familiar words, and then in such a way as to emphasize that Ahab's war is synonymous with murder. Ahab knows "all loveliness is anguish" to him, that "war is pain, and hate is woe," that he is "so far gone" on the dark side of the earth that its other side is lost to him. He recognizes himself as "demoniac . . . madness maddened." Turning aside finally from all reason, he states that he never thinks, but only "feels, feels, feels." He comes only to the verge of self-understanding at the end: "Oh, now I feel my topmost greatness lies in my topmost grief"; he does not at all comprehend the self-made causes of his pain. The correspondence Melville creates between Macbeth and Ahab implies that just as Macbeth's assessment of life as "a tale told by an idiot full of sound and fury, signifying nothing" is not Shakespeare's philosophy but his indirect expression that this is what life will come to mean to one who has negated its significance, so Ahab's destructive passion is not that of Melville, the artist, to whom creation is the great thing in life.

The images Melville uses in his portrayal strengthen the impression of Ahab as incapable of growth in his vision of, and in his relation to, life. When a poet consistently echoes a certain kind of image, above all others, in presenting a character, it is for the purpose of making a particular quality primary and the impression of it on the reader indelible. In respect to Ahab, the most emphasized trait is rigidity, always an appalling quality to Melville, as for example, in Taji or in Pierre's mother. "Iron" is the ever clanging word for Ahab. Melville makes his inflexibility available through the "clamped mortar of Ahab's iron soul," his "close-coiled woe," his "heart of wrought steel." He stands *fixed* in the pivot-hole in which his artificial leg is rooted. Much of the time he is seen motionless, wearing his "stone-carved" coat and hat, unyielding, untottering Ahab, an "iron-statue" or one of "solid bronze . . . shaped in an unalterable mould." When he speaks it is in an iron voice. What he says conveys his iron resistance to change: "The path to my fixed purpose is laid with iron rails whereon my soul is grooved to run," and his face is set like a flint toward his goal. When the compasses are inverted, he reacts with a "rigid laugh." His very suffering, though real, is rigid. Occasional moments of softening only serve to heighten by contrast the impression of essential unmalleability that precedes and follows. When, on the eve of the final chase, the *Pequod* meets the *Rachel*, whose captain pleads with Ahab to stop his hunt long enough to help search for the *Rachel*'s missing men and the captain's twelve-year-old son, Ahab, himself a father, shows emotion only when he fears the other captain will tell him that Moby Dick has been fatally wounded by the other crew, and he will be deprived of the kill. He receives the other captain's plea "icily," standing "like an anvil receiving every shock without the least quivering." His voice prolongingly molds every word: "I will not do it." Hurriedly turning, with "averted face," he descends to his cabin, leaving the *Rachel*'s captain "transfixed at this unconditional and utter rejection." His rigidity, his averted face, his walking off are, all through the narrative, visible representations of Ahab's unconditional and utter rejection not only of "God" but of man. And this rejection Melville never condones.

Rigidity characterizes not only Ahab's acts, attitudes, and purpose but also his mode of thinking. Were his imagination outreaching, like Melville's, he would not see in the whale only a reflection of his thwarted ambitions and his deprivations. He thinks, as he paces his deck, in "undeviating limits," locked in the "closed circles" of his thought. He does not really want to see more than he does, or to sort out complexities, subtleties, and interconnections, such as those he senses in Queequeg's coffin lifebuoy from which he turns, saying, "Let me not see that thing here when I return again." He does not truly want to know: he wants only to strike out at the affront of not knowing. In fact, the near prospect of striking out gives him his only moment of (sexual?) pleasure in the narrative: when he thinks he is at last about to hurl his new iron at Moby Dick, he exults, "The eternal sap runs up in Ahab's bones again." Finally his rigidity of thought and his determination to express his hatred of life by violence against it are presented, pictorially and linguistically, as two aspects of the same thing: when he darts his "fierce iron" and his far fiercer curse into the hated whale, the man, his thought, and his weapon seem one rigid welded "iron."

The others in the cast serve to illuminate Ahab's character and role. He is, like all "proud gods and commodores of the earth," one who views other men as his tools. He uses his knowledge of psychology to make his war seem theirs. He utilizes traditional forms and usages to dominate them, masking himself behind these practices and "making use of them for other and more private ends than they were legitimately intended to subserve." He waves his burning harpoon among the men, at war with them, too, if they deviate by an iota from his will. He is at war with whatever is most human in himself; he too must be his instrument. He misuses his science in the interest of his war because he has no real concern for the fate of the others, no feeling of identity with the rest of mankind; he hates whatever brings him down to the common level, whatever—time, necessity, chance, other men's needs—keeps him from being "free as air," and grasping the ungraspable. Among the men only young black Pip, and to a degree the chief mate Starbuck, are of any importance to him as human beings. But the main role of these two characters is to show Ahab turning from his "humanities." When Starbuck wants him to stop his pursuit long enough for them to fix a leak in the ship, Ahab points a loaded musket at him. When Pip wants to follow him and Ahab finds him too curing to his malady, to which he is determined to adhere, he says he will "murder" him. Some of the other characters show Ahab by contrast, and some have characteristics that highlight the poverty of his ideas and feelings by means of parody: Flask, for example, believes that the great Leviathans have personally affronted *him*.

The other main role of the rest of the crew is to show what is missing on the *Pequod*. The absolute power of rulers in the world, Melville has already implied in *White-Jacket*, depends on the consent of others to be dominated; and in the land of the war games in *Mardi* the men die in the games only because they are willing. Were there anyone in the crew of the *Pequod* to challenge effectively Ahab's power and purpose, as Mad Jack in *White-Jacket* had challenged Captain Claret's, the dynamics of the relationships and of the action in *Moby-Dick* would have to be different. If Mad Jack had been, like Starbuck, incapable of countermanding the captain's orders while knowing they would bring sure death to all, the *Neversink* and everyone on it would have perished. There is, however, a glimpse of a man whom Melville associates with the open independence of the sea and whom he shows to be a man his companions follow and miss when he is gone, his shipmates of his last voyage running after him, when he slips away on shore, with the prophetic cry, "Bulkington! where's Bulkington?" (iii, 23–24). Now, whatever Melville had in mind when he first wrote of him, in the drama as it eventually evolved, Bulkington exists only to be banished from the plot in a six-inch chapter as soon as the *Pequod* sets sail, before the men are told how Ahab means to use them. Bulkington appears to represent what is absent from the drama. Indeed, when his appearance at the Spouter Inn is related, Ishmael says that Bulkington will be his shipmate, "though but a sleeping partner one so far as this narrative is concerned" (23). Bulkington, like Queequeg, is a symbol of something fine but sleeping in the crew of man on the *Pequod*.

Starbuck, the chief mate, does question Ahab's purpose, but at no time does he challenge his authority. As the encounter with Moby Dick approaches, he stands alone outside the cabin in which Ahab is dreaming of clutching the whale's heart. The mate looks at the rack of loaded muskets, and the thought comes to him that it would not be wrong to shoot Ahab to save the lives of everyone else. An angel seems to be wrestling with him. But he replaces the musket he has picked up and leaves. On the final day the significance to Melville of the musket scene is underlined when Starbuck thinks of what Ahab is causing: "I misdoubt me that I disobey my God in obeying him." The musket scene is as close as Melville ever comes to espousing a violent solution to prevent a more widespread violence. The scene may have been one of the reasons he said to Hawthorne that he had written a wicked book about which he felt spotless as the lamb [10] (the main reason probably being that it is the "pagan" Queequeg who represents the peace and goodwill the "Christian" world preaches but in practice contradicts). But even in relation to the idea implied in the musket scene, that killing Ahab would under the circumstances be right, the last view of Starbuck in the final battle seems to say that the question of a violent solution would never arise if the Starbucks of the world would only "move, move! speak aloud!" But Starbuck vainly urges himself to do this. When all is nearly over, he asks himself, "Is this the end of . . . all my fidelities?" and Melville's implied answer is yes: Starbuck's habit of obedience to commands, no matter how mad and threatening to all, has made him an accessory in Ahab's war, as Ahab had known he would be, from the conscription scene on the quarterdeck on: "Aye, aye, thy silence, then, *that* voices thee . . . Starbuck now is mine" (xxxvi, 144).

Ishmael sees the mariners and castaways of the crew as morally enfeebled by the "mere unaided virtue" of Starbuck, the reckless indifference to life of the second mate, and the pervading mediocrity of the third (xli, 162). Although the men have the potentialities hinted by Ishmael, whose God throws "one royal mantle of humanity over all'" (xxvi, 105), these are dormant. Leaderless, isolated from each other, trained to mechanical observance of the forms and usages, they are, Ishmael says, as if picked to follow Ahab, whose war purpose so domineers above them that all their doubts hide beneath their souls and do "not sprout forth a single spear or leaf" (cxxx, 437–38).

Among all the characters only one, Queequeg, is placed by Melville in effective opposition to Ahab. It is not a narrative opposition, achieved dramatically, but an artistic opposition achieved by poetic means. Ahab and Queequeg stand in contrast, not in active conflict, with each other. It may be said that in respect to his role in the work there are two Queequegs (as in *Othello* there are two scales of time), one the "character" who is a member of the harpooning trio and participant in the drama as a part of Ahab's obedient machine, the other the symbol of the life-preserving immortal spirit that can save man, as the life-negating Ahab spirit would destroy him.

In Queequeg Melville gives physical form to his conception, first expressed in *Typee* and last in *Billy Budd,* of an original peaceful and creative possibility in man, which has survived in spite of all the corruptions of the "all-grasping western world" (lxxxvii, 318). Melville conveys Queequeg's nature in extraordinarily visual ways, revealing him as one in whom there is no separation between ideas and acts, appearance and reality, as Melville felt there was in the civilization of his day.

Queequeg's fantastic appearance imparts the understanding that he is not to be taken as a man of any one time, place, or color. In him seemingly incongruous things are juxtaposed and combined. His complexion is of a dark purplish, yellow color, here and there stuck over with large, blackish squares. "Who could show a cheek like Queequeg? which, barred with various tints, seemed like the Andes' western slope, *to show forth in one array, contrasting climates, zone by zone*" (my emphasis). His body, too, is checkered with various colors, and his legs are marked "as if a parcel of dark green frogs were running up the trunks of young palms": like the whale, Queequeg unites all life—human, other animal, and plant. His arm is tattooed all over with an "interminable Cretan labyrinth of a figure, no two parts of which were of one precise shade." The place he comes from is not on any map. Melville links him to many people, ages, and places: to far-off tribes; Zoroaster; the ancient Babylonians, Greeks, and Egyptians; the South Seas and the Congo; to whatever, anywhere, ever, may have been valuable in the interpretation of life and can aid in man's survival through a marriage of cultures. *This* is what is implicit in the embrace and "marriage" of Queequeg and Ishmael. Those who see this marriage as, literally, a homosexual union miss the poet's conceptual image. Queequeg is a man in peaceful relation to his fellow man, as he is to the universe and to himself—in contrast to solipsistic, self-alienated Ahab who is out of relation to all.[11]

In spite of the fact that Queequeg as part of the magnetized crew and Queequeg as symbol are not fused, in the evenly spaced incidents in which he acts to save life, his role as character and as image *are* in focus, and these are scenes that stand out in the memory like unforgettable shots in a great film. These scenes appear throughout but most regularly as the work approaches its climax. All of them highlight his poise, his immortal health, and his sense of responsibility to man and life: his "long living arc of a leap" to rescue from drowning the bumpkin who has mimicked him; his deliverance, "or rather delivery," of Tashtego; his rescue of the ship when it is being capsized by the sinking whale lashed to it, slashing with a heavy hammer at the largest fluke chains that link all in the crew to needless death; his descent into the hold and his crawling about in the cold and slime to discover the leak; and his resulting fever that makes him look all frame and tattooing, everything else fading away but his eyes "rounding and rounding like the rings of Eternity." He is the image and essence "in one array" of all the incorrupt and peaceful things Ishmael speaks of at intervals: the incorruptibility in the midst of decay; the Tahiti in man's soul; that "immaculate manliness we feel within ourselves, so far within us, that it remains intact though all the outer character seem gone"; and "whatever is truly wondrous . . . in man."

Though he cares about preserving the lives of others, Queequeg is calm at the thought of his own death, since it is his belief that after it he will sail out into the universe. But, remembering a duty he is leaving undone ashore, he decides not to die just then and to use as a sea chest the canoe he has had made to be his coffin. He carves its lid with figures copied from the hieroglyphics tattooed on his body. These set forth a theory concerning the heavens and earth and the mystical art of attaining truth. When Ahab senses that Queequeg embodies something of great significance, he turns from that meaning, as he soon afterward turns away from the canoe-coffin that Queequeg offers as a lifebuoy to replace the old one, which has become useless (as if the old values meant to protect life have been proved useless): Ahab, the miracle worker who can reset the needles of the compass so that they may again lead to war and destruction, has no power to fix the lifebuoy; only Queequeg, the "pagan" savior, can provide the life preserver that in the end, after the ship is pulled down, shoots out of the vortex and saves Ishmael, suggesting the umbilical connection between death and life that Ahab sensed in the coffin preserver but refused to consider. Ishmael, sustained by what is usually a symbol of death, comes out of the disaster as if reborn. The coffin has become a "cradle."

Now we see that Ishmael is not only the narrator-commentator who can tell the story from inside the action, but that he, too, is a poetic symbol—mankind saved from annihilation to have another chance at life. In Ishmael, as in humanity, opposing influences have been at work. There is a time in the narrative when he is utterly under the sway of Ahab, accepting Ahab's feud as his own, sensing nothing in Moby Dick but evil, and welding his oath "of violence and revenge" with the oaths Ahab draws from the others. And there is a later time when, suffused with the spirit of shared life and peace, he squeezes his co-laborers' hands, as together they work the hardening spermaceti, bringing back its lifelike fluidity, and, in this joint activity, forgets his horrible oath: "in that inexpressible sperm, I washed my hands and heart of it." Saved from the nearly total extinction of life on the *Pequod,* Ishmael lives to tell what is essentially the story of the death of a god, the death of an age doomed to destruction because of its warmaking goals and the tragic waste of its knowledge and energy and life. It will be for Ishmael, man's representative to the future from the wreck of the past, to explore the meaning of his experience and create a new conception of man's (not God's or Fate's) responsibility for the nature and goal of his life, a new concept of "God" he will continually have to re-create in the manner of Queequeg continually whittling his wooden image.[12]

The narrator of *Moby-Dick* is the new Ishmael in the process of searching out the meaning of his experience. This Ishmael feels he must speak aloud in the interest of humanity. In his love of Queequeg he rejects, tacitly, the idea that the world must forever be to man (as to the old sailor from the Isle of Man) a fighting ring bound by the horizon, the ring in which Cain struck Abel. The Ishmael who had begun, like Ahab, hating life, with "splintered heart and maddened hand . . . turned against the wolfish world," turns in the end, so unlike Ahab, from his *in*humanities. He sees that it is a "devil's chase" in which he has been implicated. He has come to see himself as part, and only a part, of man, and in this way, too, he is now at the opposite philosophical pole from Ahab. But though he now sees his life as a particle in a continuum, he has come to care more about it. He sees the danger, as in looking back on his first watch at the masthead, of being so lost in the abstract and infinite that identity is lost, spirit is "diffused through time and space," and "there is no life in thee." Melville, through this new Ishmael, envisions individual life and Life in relation.

Although most of the ideas Ishmael expresses can be taken to be Melville's, Ishmael is, of course, not the poet in whose imagination all, including the narrator, was conceived. But he is Melville's most intimate incarnation, and his experience is a symbolic transfiguration of Melville's own. For Melville, like Ishmael, had been a wanderer who learned about life and death and the world of war in his travels. Like Ishmael (and in some ways like that other traveler Jonah,[13] and like White-Jacket, too), Melville had to "descend" into the midst of the seas to find whatever part of life's truths might be available to him as one man in one time. He knew what Ahablike things had proved menacing to him and to others in his wanderings; he knew what Queequeglike ideals had upheld him. He had, in his earlier works, tried to analyze the world in which war was "the greatest of evils."[14] Although in *Moby-Dick* the knowledge he had gained was transmuted into a more complex poetry than before, he did not change his analysis of "the true condition of the present civilization of the world,"[15] and man's choice between war and peace remained to him fundamental for the future civilization of the world. However, the context of the world of the present enlarged: the *Pequod*, the crew, and the whale are part of one great drama in space and time. In the nineteenth-century act of the drama, which we see in *Moby-Dick*, the crew and the whale are in conflict. The human participants are bound within the circle of the chase, wherein the pursuer is pursued. What will happen in the next act or acts? Suggested by the imagery and by the narrative is the idea that what follows will depend, above all, on whether man can bring forth a new design of life to replace the rigid circle of the chase to which he has been "enslaved." Even the shape of *Moby-Dick* expresses this: the narrative movement that has proceeded in accordance with Ahab's determination to chase the white whale "round" Good Hope, and "round" the Horn, and "round" the Norway Maelstrom, and "round" perdition's flames, continues to almost the very end and then breaks out of the narrowing circle. The ship has gone down; and Ishmael, who has been floating on the margin of the scene, is drawn toward the closing vortex: "Round and round, then, and ever-contracting toward the button-like black bubble of the axis of that slowly wheeling circle, like another Ixion I did revolve. Till, gaining that vital centre, the black bubble upward burst; and now, liberated by reason of its cunning spring, and, owing to its great buoyancy, rising with great force, the coffin life-buoy shot lengthwise from the sea, fell over, and floated by my side." Man, the image suggests, will be another Ixion bound to a revolving wheel of fire until he is released by the spirit to which Queequeg's buoyant coffin lifebuoy gives form. Ishmael, upheld by the coffin, is picked up by the "devious-cruising" *Rachel*, her movement, too, a contrast with the *Pequod*'s.

Every great work of literature has meaning beyond its time. *Moby-Dick* seems prophetic of ours, foreseeing the possibility of total destruction resulting from unrestrained war: "And now, concentric circles seized the lone boat itself, and all its crew, and each floating oar, and every lance-pole, and, spinning, animate and inanimate, all round and round in one vortex, carried the smallest chip of the Pequod out of sight." But there is, too, the possibility symbolized by the rising canoe-coffin that gives life to a new Ishmael, to a new, more human, being. Buoyed up by it he floats on the creamy pool into which the turmoil has subsided, and the world, for the symbolic moment, is stunningly transformed: "The unharming sharks, they glided by as if with padlocks on their mouths; the savage sea-hawks sailed with sheathed beaks." And with this memorable surrealistic image to pictorialize the idea of a transformed and peaceful world, Melville ends his, and world literature's, great symbolic poem of war and peace.

Notes

1. From January 1841 to May 1843.
2. *Mardi* (Evanston, Ill.: Northwestern Univ. Press and The Newberry Library, 1970), Chs. i–ii, pp. 3–10.
3. "Textual Problems of *Moby-Dick,*" pp. 471–77, in the Norton Critical Edition of the work, gives a succinct account by the editors, Harrison Hayford and Hershel Parker, of the facts known about the first and second stage in its composition.
4. The metaphor of tides moving back and forth in a work of fiction as it grows is taken from a letter by Wilson Harris in specific reference to his *Tree of the Sun* (London: Faber and Faber, 1978), but it must, I think, describe the way in which any long work of the imagination develops in the course of composition.
5. *Moby-Dick* (New York: Norton, 1967), Ch. xli, p. 156. All references in the text and in the notes will be to this edition.
6. In Melville's imagination, prosecution of war is repeatedly associated with madness. "Bridegroom Dick" spells it out: "But avast with the War! Why recall racking days / . . . It irks me now, as it troubled me then, / To think o' the fate in the madness o' men."
7. In this paragraph the chapter and page references are as follows: "thing of trophies," Ch. xvi, p. 67; "like a javelin . . . ," Ch. xcix, p. 358; "as captains of companies," Ch. xxvi, p. 106; "the long line of man-of-war's men . . . ," Ch. xlvii, pp. 186–87; "marching . . . first battle," Ch. xlviii, p. 193.
8. In this paragraph and the six that follow, all concerning the significance in the narrative of the whale in his "broad genera" and in his most dramatic manifestation in Moby Dick, the chapter and page references are as follows: "king of creation," Ch. civ, p. 380; "largest inhabitant," Ch. xxxii, p. 120; "mass . . . life," Ch. lxxvi, p. 285; "surplus stock of vitality," Ch. lxxxv, p. 311; "immortal in his species," Ch. cv, p. 384; "the Deity and the dread powers," Ch. lxxix, p. 292; "waning world," Ch. lxxxi, p. 301; "whale and sun dying together," Ch. cxvi, p. 409; "very pelvis of the world," Ch. xxxii, p. 118; "chance-like apparition of life," Ch. lix, p. 237; "headwaters of the Eternities," Ch. cv, p. 381; "swam the seas," Ch. cv, p. 384; "so wide a chase," Ch. cv, p. 383; "mightiest animated mass," Ch. xiv, p. 62; "the eternal whale," Ch. cv, p. 385; "ubiquitous," Ch. xli, p. 158; "left his wake," Ch. civ, p. 380; concerning the skeleton on the island, Ch. cii, pp. 374–75; whale defying classification, and whale "scientific or poetic," Ch. xxxii, pp. 123, 118; "Dissect him how I may," Ch. lxxxvi, p. 318; "his life . . . indiscer-

nible hills," Ch. lxxxi, p. 301; how interpretation of the whale varies; Ch. lxxxvi, p. 317; "one grand hooded phantom" and the "ungraspable phantom of life," Ch. i, pp. 16, 14; "all the horrors of the half-known life," Ch. lviii, p. 236.

9. In this paragraph and the five that follow, all concerning Melville's methods of portraying Ahab, the chapter and page references are as follows: "narrow-flowing monomania," Ch. xli, p. 161; God seen by Ahab as a murderer, Ch. cxxxii, p. 445; "in his heart," Ch. xli, p. 161; "Commend the murderous chalices," Ch. xxxvi, p. 146; "all loveliness is anguish," Ch. xxxvii, p. 147; "war is pain," Ch. cxix, p. 417; "so far gone," Ch. cxxvii, p. 433; "demoniac . . . madness maddened," Ch. xxxvii, p. 147; "feels, feels, feels," Ch. cxxxv, p. 460; "clamped mortar," Ch. cxxx, p. 438; "close-coiled woe," Ch. cxxxii, p. 442; "heart of wrought steel," Ch. cxxxv, p. 463; "solid bronze," Ch. xxviii, p. 110; "path to my fixed purpose," Ch. xxxvii, p. 147; "rigid laugh," Ch. cxxiv, p. 424; the rejection of the Rachel's captain's plea, Ch. cxxviii, p. 435; "Let me not see that thing," Ch. cxxvii, p. 433; "The eternal sap runs up," Ch. cxxxiii, p. 451; "proud gods and commodores," Ch. ix, p. 51; Ahab's masking himself behind the forms, "making use of them," Ch. xxxiii, p. 129; "free as air," Ch. cviii, p. 392; Flask believing Leviathans have personally affronted *him,* Ch. xxvii, p. 106.

10. Letter to Hawthorne, November 1851.

11. In this paragraph and the two that follow, all dealing with Queequeg's appearance, actions, and beliefs, the chapter and page references are as follows: "Who could show a cheek like Queequeg," Ch. v, p. 36; "as if a parcel of dark green frogs," Ch. iii, p. 29; "Cretan labyrinth," Ch. iv, p. 32; Queequeg saving the bumpkin, Ch. xiii, p. 61; "delivery" of Tashtego, Ch. lxxviii, pp. 288–90; slashing the fluke chains, Ch. lxxxi, pp. 302–3; Queequeg's descent into the hold, Ch. cx, p. 395; Queequeg's eyes like rings of Eternity, Ch. cx, p. 395; "immaculate manliness," Ch. xxvi, p. 104; "whatever is truly wondrous," Ch. cx, p. 396; theory of heaven and earth, Ch. cx, p. 399; Ahab turning from markings on Queequeg's body, Ch. cx, p. 399; Ahab turning from the coffin lifebuoy, Ch. cxxvii, p. 433.

12. In this paragraph and the one that follows, chapter and page references are as follows: oath of "violence and revenge," Ch. xli, p. 155; forgets his horrible oath, Ch. xciv, p. 348; "with splintered heart," Ch. x, p. 53; "devil's chase," Ch. xlix, p. 196; the masthead experience, Ch. xxxv, pp. 134–40.

13. In some ways Father Mapple's sermon on Jonah has implications for Ishmael and Melville; in other ways Jonah is connected to Ahab, the most fascinating of them being the "slouched hat" that Melville has both wear; references to Ahab's "slouched hat" are so important to Melville's picture of him that he wears it (Ch. cxxxii, p. 443) even after the hawk has flown off with it and after "The Hat" chapter says, "Ahab's hat was never restored" Ch. cxxx, p. 441). Or could Melville have made this "mistake" deliberately, to call attention to the symbolic nature of the slouched hat as the mark of one who defies "God"?

14. *Omoo* (Evanston, Ill.: Northwestern Univ. Press and The Newberry Library, 1968), Ch. xxix, p. 108n.

15. *White-Jacket* (Evanston, Ill.: Northwestern Univ. Press and The Newberry Library, 1970), Ch. lxx, p. 293.

5.

Israel Potter: The American Revolution and the Forgotten Man

For him our Revolution was in vain.

—*White-Jacket,* xxxv

In London to arrange for the English edition of *White-Jacket,* Melville wrote in his journal on December 18, 1849, that he had bought a 1776 map of the city "in case I serve up the Revolutionary narrative of the beggar." [1] The narrative that had caught his interest because of its historical and social implications was the autobiography of an impoverished veteran of the American Revolution who had had it printed in 1824 as part of his effort to gain a pension. The story of Israel Potter, volunteer soldier and sailor, who did not reap the benefits of the Revolution he helped to win, whose hardships in war were followed by poverty for long years in England and continuation of poverty back in America, and who had no one but himself to relate his history, must have struck Melville as illustrating two of his convictions: one, that for many Americans the Revolution had been in vain, and the other, that in any war the common sailors and soldiers—upon whom "kings" rely for power, military officers for "glory," and "Commerce" for profit—experience the greatest hardships and die unrewarded and forgotten. [2] The biblical connotations of the author's name must at once have suggested to Melville, always alert to such associations and to irony, thoughts of an Israel to whom the promised land ever

79

remained a dream and whose only reward was to rest in peace in some "potter's field."

As finally interpreted in *Israel Potter: His Fifty Years of Exile* (1855),[3] the humble hero's life is, from early youth to death and oblivion, symbolic of the fate of the "plebian" heroes of the Revolution, and his exile becomes, by the end, more than geographical. The narrative took on universal overtones, Israel coming to represent also the poor in any land who in peace give "cosy seats to all the rest of the world" (xxvi, 262) and in war provide the bodies on which officers climb to fame—an idea pictorialized when Israel literally serves as a ladder for John Paul Jones (xvi, 163). The future of the United States is not predicted: instead three possibilities are set forth by means of three famous Americans whom Melville has Israel encounter.

Each major section of *Israel Potter* contributes to the imaginative presentation of Melville's philosophy of the Revolution, as of war in general, in relation to the poor. The development is chronological, but the ideas underlying the main divisions of Israel's life are closely interwoven.

The dedication, dated June 17, 1854, the anniversary of the Battle of Bunker Hill in which Israel fought, is an integral part of the work. It is addressed to "His Highness, the Bunker-Hill Monument," the only "Great Biographer" of the "anonymous privates of June 17, 1775." With the irony and understatement that characterize the whole dedication, the "Editor" censures the way America's Revolutionary history has been told: that Israel's name has not appeared in the volumes written by Jared Sparks "may or may not be a matter for astonishment."

A Melville prelude opens the narrative. Its description of Israel's birthplace and its recital of the experience of his youth predict what is to come. Spring in the Berkshire Hills, followed by autumn bleak and sere and winter when all is blocked with snow, is a foretaste of "the fresh early tints of the spring of 1776," to be followed for Israel by nearly half a century of bleak years in England and then a return home to find that every path he takes is blocked. His hopes, when he emancipates himself from his unreasonable father, are frustrated, as will be those he has when he helps throw off the yoke of the king on "just principles." And just as his desires to wed the girl he loves are not "crowned with fruition," since when he returns from his early journeys the "dear, false girl" is "another's," so his later desires remain unconsummated; what has held out promise is false to him; the fair things for which he has struggled are enjoyed only by others.

The body of the book begins when Israel volunteers and in the Battle of Bunker Hill receives a long slit across the chest. It is a scar later to be traversed by a cutlass wound in a sea battle, making him, in the end—as common soldier and sailor in one body—the "bescarred bearer of a cross" (xxvii, 270). Soon after his first wound he volunteers to help man one of the American boats. The vessel is captured and he is taken to England as a prisoner, but he escapes and, after many hardships, meets a group of patriotic Englishmen who find the war against the colonies monstrous and who send him as a courier to Benjamin Franklin in Paris. Through Franklin he meets John Paul Jones.

These famous Americans appear in a light quite different from the one in which the average history books present them. Each personifies a spirit that may, alone or in alliance with the other, dominate and corrupt the future United States.

Franklin is the embodiment of the purely materialist values that Melville repeatedly portrays as standing in the way of America's professed political, social, and religious ideals. He is the "type and genius of his land," able to turn whatever and whomever he encounters to a profit. He offers Israel the promise of a passage home but, having other uses for him, snatches it away the next moment, making the exile feel "as though a plum-pudding had been thrust under his nostrils, and then as rapidly withdrawn" (vii, 65). The promised land, Melville hints, cannot be reached through what Franklin, or his philosophy, has to offer.

Nor can it be reached through what John Paul Jones represents. Franklin, who is prepared to use Jones, knows that his spirit is invaluable in war "as projectiles and combustibles" (x, 93). A human explosive, he is fired by a rage for glory. In the voice of "a prophecy" Melville warns, "intrepid, unprincipled, reckless, predatory, with boundless ambition, civilized in externals but a savage at heart, America is, or may yet be, the Paul Jones of nations" (xix, 192).

The events in which Jones moves like "a crimson thread" across the fabric of Israel's life make up a third of the work (xiv–xx, 139–213)). The section presents, almost entirely by narrative and poetic means, two themes from *White-Jacket:* that so far from being glorious, war is butchery, and that the fame it holds out as a lure is not for the common man: like all the "plum-pudding" promises to Israel, it does not materialize: "This cruise made loud fame for Paul. . . . But poor Israel, who also had conquered a craft, and all unaided, too—what had he?" (xvii, 182).

The carnage depicted in the two-chapter unit that vividly paints the fight between the British ship *Serapis* and Jones's *Bonhomme Richard* would be unimaginable to the reader who has never experienced battle were it not made so intensely visualizable in this best section of the book. It is strange that this sea battle account should be called by Raymond Weaver "one of the most glamorous in all the literatures of the sea" ("Introduction"), for it is the extreme contrast between the seeming glamor of the scene as viewed from a distance and its actuality when seen up close that is the essence of the pair of chapters, each numbered xix. Melville's way of showing this contrast is an instance of how his hatred of war inspired boldly original artistic techniques at one with the ideas they develop. The movement of the account of this battle is inward: from distant appearance to inner reality; from the romantic view seen by thousands of "distant spectators crowning the high cliffs of Yorkshire" to the close view necessary to "possess" the events; from a scene that Turner might have painted [4] to a series of shockingly realistic pictures that the Goya of *The Disasters of War* might have drawn.

In the view of the distant onlookers the reality of the battle is obscured by a cloud foaming with fire and by a vapor suffused with golden light from a full moon low on the horizon whose rays light but do not "pierce" the haze. But the glamorous effect is a deception created by "Mephistopheles, prompter of the stage," pleased to see how well his "charms" work. The deceptive "cloud" has to be pierced: "To get some idea of the events enacting in that cloud, it will be necessary to enter it." The "inside" view is a series of devastating details: the ships are interlocked; the rigging of each is ablaze; marksmen at the tops, with arms or legs broken, fall from their perches "like falling pigeons shot on the wing"; cannon bursting apart explode the soldiers working them and shatter part of the hull; men "in transports of intrepidity" strip themselves naked and expose their bodies to the shots; fire igniting heaped cartridges runs "like an express on a railway" killing twenty men; the main hatchway of the *Serapis* is a "slaughterous pit."

Through Jones in this battle, Melville presents his equation of war, Satan, and sin. When Jones, the very spirit of war, whose intent it is to "inspirit and madden his men," lays back his gold-laced sleeve, the blue tattooing on his arm is disclosed, "cabalistically terrific as the charmed standard of Satan," and when his ship succumbs to fire and water and the crew take over the *Serapis*, the *Bonhomme Richard* "gorged with slaughter, wallowed heavily, gave a long roll, and blasted by tornadoes of sulphur, slowly sunk, like Gomorrah, out of sight."

The section featuring John Paul ends when Israel is literally, as he has all along been figuratively, carried away by the warmaking spirit instilled in him by Jones. He leaps upon the deck of an enemy ship, is borne away by her when she makes a fast getaway, and is taken back again to England, though, by his ingenuity (and Melville's humor), not as a prisoner. Landed in Falmouth, he strolls past Pendennis Castle and hears the voice of a prisoner, "as of the roar of some tormented lion."

In this way, through his voice, Melville introduces the American, Ethan Allen, whose spirit he offers as the only truly promising alternative to the materialistic spirit of his Franklin and the warmaking spirit of his Jones. His portrayal of Allen expresses his belief, of greatest importance in *White-Jacket* and *Moby-Dick*, that speaking up against oppression is a human being's responsibility and that words, were they only used, could serve instead of weapons. Allen, in *Israel Potter*, is, above all, "articulate." The scene in the castle yard is dominated by his voice speaking up for freedom, which he values more than any other thing. That he (who, Melville knew, did not espouse Christianity) is a "true gentleman and Christian" while his captors are "Turks" is his loud refrain. Melville, in his one detour from narration, interprets Allen's symbolic meaning in *Israel Potter*. Never quietly submissive to abuse, his thunderous voice alone, directed against those who would oppress him, is enough to "shock them into retreat." Only when he is

menaced does he fight, not taking the mere malice of his foes too
seriously. His is not the New England spirit (dominated by old
England) but is "essentially Western." In the context of the whole
Ethan Allen section this spirit is a combination of love of freedom,
courage in the face of adversity, humor, bold exercise of freedom of
speech, readiness to try what has not yet been done, willingness to
depart from old values and theologies, and practice of just principles. Unlike the spirit of Franklin or Jones, Allen's is the pioneering
spirit, bold in exploring the new.

In the four chapters that complete the tale of Israel's sufferings
in England, London and its environs represent the hell to which
the poor, especially the urban and milltown "laboring classes" are
everywhere condemned. Outstanding among the realities of desti-
tution as Israel experiences it for forty-five years in London is the
"Malthusian enigma" that those of the poor who survive seem able
to hold on to their lives only because of death-bringing war. Making use of events reported in the original autobiography, Melville
looks into a fact he has not before examined, and, eighty-five years
before Brecht's *Mother Courage,* brings home to the reader the bitter
fact that in supposedly civilized and Christian lands there are
many, like Israel, so poor that for them each outbreak of war is an
"encouragement," each return of peace a calamity (xxvi, 262–64).
After the war, hordes of disbanded soldiers compete for work.
Then Israel's lot is "relieved" when the war with France breaks out
in 1793 and work becomes available. "In 1817 he once more en-
dured extremity; this second peace again drifting its discharged
soldiers on London, so that all kinds of labor were overstocked." By
an implied comparison between the rich and certain beggars who
pretend to have fought and been wounded, Melville hints that the
"crafty aristocracy . . . without having endangered their own per-
sons much if anything, reaped no insignificant share both of the
glory and profit of the bloody battles they claimed; while some of
the genuine working heroes, too brave to beg, too cut-up to work,
and too poor to live, laid down quietly in corners and died." In
spite of everything, however, sturdy, ingenious Israel, "our wandering Jew," survives.

Because of poverty, only he and his youngest son remain alive
out of a family of thirteen. Throughout his exile abroad Israel has

dreamed of America. But, hinting at how his "Revolutionary narrative" will end, Melville calls Israel's vision of the beauties and "shared" plenty of his homeland a "sort of hallucination" and has the boy listen to "tales of the Fortunate Isles of the Free" as to "the stories of Sinbad the Sailor." When he grows up, the son, filled with the desire to go with his now very old father to America, at last wins the help of the American consul.

The last chapter, "Requiescat in Pace," is a coda rounding out the theme of exile in the fullest sense. When Israel lands in Boston on the Fourth of July, 1826, he is almost "run over by a patriotic triumphal car in the procession, flying a broidered banner, inscribed with *gilt* letters: 'BUNKER-HILL! 1775 / GLORY TO THE HEROES THAT FOUGHT!' " (my emphasis). Israel and his son journey to Israel's birthplace. There no one knows him or can "recall having heard of him." Three-fourths of his old neighbors have moved westward, including the only survivor in his family. His early home long ago burned down. Wandering in the wilderness still, he sees a moldy pile of wood, through whose decay the crumbling of the strong but not imperishable early Revolutionary ideals is intimated:

> Though wherever touched by his staff, however lightly, this pile would crumble, yet here and there, even in powder, it preserved the exact look, each irregularly defined line, of what it had originally been—namely, a half-cord of stout hemlock (one of the woods least affected by exposure to the air), in a foregoing generation chopped and stacked up on the spot, against sledging-time, but, as sometimes happens in such cases, by subsequent oversight, abandoned to oblivious decay—type now, as it stood there, of forever arrested intentions, and a long life still rotting in early mishap. (xxvii, 272)

Israel's spirit is not given to despair. He encounters a hardworking farmer of a later generation (a new symbol of the poor) whose plow has year after year been halted by the half-buried hearth of the home of which Israel has dreamed, and his advice is, "Plough away, friend." The rest of the story is quickly told: "He was repulsed in efforts after a pension by certain caprices of law. His scars proved his only medals. He dictated a little book, the record of his fortunes. But long ago it faded out of print—himself out of being—his name out of memory. He died the same day that the oldest oak in his native hills was blown down." So the hemlock and oak that in "Misgivings" in *Battle-Pieces* will shake in the rafter and keel are, figuratively, here, too, the strong but not strong enough material of which the country was made. The early intentions of the Revolution have been "forever arrested."

Israel Potter: His Fifty Years of Exile does not imply that the Revolution should not have taken place. It finds it inevitable: as Israel's father's tyranny caused his son's emancipation, so British oppression inexorably brought the Revolution. What the work dramatizes is the irony that in the lives of the poor no revolution whatsoever has occurred. In the period that is, by the time Israel dies, well over half a century, the United States has been for symbolic Israel Potter only a *new* England. What the future intentions of the country will be—whether its spirit will be that of Jones or Franklin or Allen—is not predicted. But what ought to help shape more truly revolutionary intentions, the narrative as a whole conveys, is the knowledge that the hardworking plebian heroes upon whom the nation has always relied for its existence have been too long forgotten in history and in life. Israel Potter is Melville's memorial to those he pictured as still in "exile" from their country's thought and from the gains of the American Revolution.

Notes

1. Merton M. Sealts, Jr., *Melville's Reading* (Madison: Univ. of Wisconsin Press, 1966), p. 86, No. 407.
2. For direct expressions of these ideas in works written by Melville before 1849 see: (1) *Mardi's* takeoff on the Declaration of Independence (Ch. clvii); (2) *Mardi's* account of the war games (Chs. cxxxvii–xliii); (3) *Redburn's* description of the Nelson statuary (Ch. xxxi); (4) *Redburn's* suggestion that the Liverpool docks should be named after men like Nelson and Rodney so that their names might fittingly be perpetuated "in connection with the commerce they defended" (Ch. xxii); (5) *Redburn's* reactions to the army recruiting posters (Ch. xi); (6) *White-Jacket's* contrasts between the interests of the officers and the common sailors in time of war (Ch. xlix); and (7) *White-Jacket* on the

common sailor for whom "our Revolution was in vain" and the Declaration of Independence a lie (Ch. xxxv).

3. All references in this chapter are to Raymond Weaver's edition of *Israel Potter* (New York: A. & C. Boni, 1924).

4. Turner's *The Fighting Temeraire,* with its low-lying moon and softly colored mist, hiding details, may have been in Melville's mind when he wrote this description. On page 224 of Hennig Cohen's edition of *Battle-Pieces* is a picture captioned, "Melville owned an engraving by James T. Willmore after painting, 'The Fighting Temeraire.' "

6.

Benito Cereno: Slavery and Violence in the Americas

An oracle for the United States before the Civil War, with resonating meaning for all of humanity, *Benito Cereno* (1855) [1] has been, like many a legendary oracle, misconceived by those who expect meaning to be conveyed in conventional ways. The assumption has been that Melville in this work borrowed the old symbolism of black as evil, white as good. Out of this has grown the common interpretation that Babo—leader of the black slave revolt on the *San Dominick*—is symbolic of Evil; that Don Benito Cereno—captain of the ship transporting slaves and friend from youth of the slave-owner—is the good victim of "black" iniquity; that Captain Amasa Delano of Massachusetts—who never seriously questions the enslavement of blacks and unconsciously accepts its rationale, who sees at all times only what is visible on the surface, and who learns nothing from the *San Dominick* experience, which he recommends forgetting—is innocence discovering Evil; and that slavery—without which there could be no *Benito Cereno*—is irrelevant to the story.

But Melville was a poet—maker, not taker, of symbols, methods, and forms. His head, being like Babo's a "hive of subtlety," he transformed the 1817 narrative written by a real Amasa Delano [2] into strange suggestive art through which he explored, more deeply and creatively than ever before, the master-slave relationship and the entanglement of slavery and violence; though he felt here, as everywhere else in his works, that the great iniquity resides in slavery, not in those who fight, no matter how bloodily, against it, he was impelled by the extraordinary situation recounted in the source to probe as profoundly as possible "horrors that happen so." [3]

Far from developing his thought in glaring black and white, Melville beclouded it, challenging American readers to "pierce" [4] in this work, as they needed to in life, the surface and also the upper substratum of slavery in order to arrive at its skeletal reality. In harmony with this purpose, his imagination brought forth entirely original artistic conceptions. The work is a series of palimpsestlike pictures. Layers of irony underlie obvious ironies. Skeletons (human, ship, animal) imply the existence of innermost realities. There are hints of unseen "interiors." Shadows foreshadow; past, present, and future are merged. A fate for the United States akin to that of Spain in the Americas is conveyed through masked symbols. The sun is "screened"; brightness is "eclipsed." And the black and the white figures act as complex dialectical opposites, not unsubtle moral extremes, in a relationship as imprisoning as the "oaken walls" of the *San Dominick,* as contradictory as the situation that puzzles Delano, and as fraught with violence as the seemingly peaceful scene the North American captain fails to understand.

The arrangement of the work, too, implies an interior reality covered over by layers of misconceptions or mere facts. The story is presented in three parts, all objectively narrated. The opening section, read for the first time, seems to present only the facts as they unfold to Delano. The second, the deposition Don Benito gives to the court, provides the background. The third demands that readers think, after the story ends, about what is still missing, go back to the beginning, and try to penetrate to the underlying form and process of which this story is a fascinating instance. What happens in *Benito Cereno* is more a matter of what is hinted than what is told. For that reason a different kind of "plot" summary from the usual review of events alone is needed as the basis for my analysis of this work's fusion of art and thought.

The year is 1799, the place the waters off a small uninhabited island near the southern tip of South America. Captain Delano, whose ship, a combination of sealer and general trader, has anchored at the island for water, sees a "strange sail"—one gets the impression of a phantom ship—showing "no colors." All things are gray; gray fowl skim overhead "as swallows over meadows before storms," and everywhere are "Shadows present, foreshadowing deeper shadows to come." Seeing that the ship is in distress, Captain Delano lowers his whaleboat so that he may board the vessel and help to bring it in. As he approaches, it looks like a "whitewashed" monastery. This is the first of a number of strange metaphors that place in juxtaposition the ship carrying masters and slaves and such structures as "superannuated Italian palaces . . . under a decline of masters" (241) and "the charred ruin of some summer-house in a grand garden long running to waste" (269), associations that seem farfetched and arbitrary until one sees that what links them is the idea of pretended value or past power, of social edifices that are skeletons of their "former state" or ghostly indications of their imminent collapse.

When he comes closer, Delano recognizes the ship as a Spanish merchantman carrying Negro slaves "amongst other valuable freight" from one colonial port to another. Once a frigate of the Spanish king's navy, "In the present business in which she was engaged, the ship's general model and rig appeared to have undergone no material change from their original warlike . . . pattern." (Here, as more openly in *White-Jacket* and *Billy Budd*, the ship of war and the ship of enslavement are one.) An oval sternpiece carved with the arms of Castile and León shows a dark satyr in a mask who holds his foot on the "prostrate" neck of a "writhing" figure also masked. Whether the ship has a figurehead is not clear to Captain Delano as he nears the *San Dominick*, for a canvas covers the bow, below which has been rudely painted "Seguid vuestro jefe" (Follow your leader). The name of the ship appears in corroded letters, once gilt.

Delano finds a crowd on board in which blacks, including women, outnumber whites more than is usual on a slave transportation ship. All tell a tale of death by storms and illness. Six black hatchet polishers are seated on an elevated poop and to Delano have "the raw aspect of unsophisticated Africans." Turning to see who is in command, he has his initial view of ill Don Benito and Babo—the first in a long series of tableaux featuring master and slave—and through Delano's early thought about the two, Melville subtly points to the phenomenon his work will explore: "As master and man stood before him, the black upholding the white, Captain Delano could not but bethink him of the beauty of that *relationship* which could present such a spectacle of fidelity on the one hand and confidence on the other. The scene was heightened by the contrast in dress, denoting their *relative* positions" (250; my emphasis).

As the day advances certain things make Delano uneasy: a lack of openness on the part of Don Benito, puzzling aspects of the story he tells, and odd behavior on the part of the crew. Don Benito explains that the slaves are unfettered, since their owner had said that with "his blacks" chains would be unnecessary. But one giant, Atufal, has an iron collar around his neck with a chain thrice wound around his body and a padlock at his waist. Delano is told that until Atufal asks Don Benito's pardon for some unnamed offense the chains must remain, but the Spanish captain has not been able to break down "the entrenched will of the slave." Feelings of security and insecurity ebb and flow in Delano. He feels vaguely that the *San Dominick*, "like a slumbering volcano," may "suddenly let loose energies now hid"—the very image of violence building up because of slavery that will reappear in "The Apparition" in *Battle-Pieces*. He does not suspect the blacks of any plot because he thinks they are by nature "too stupid" (270), but Don Benito's behavior seems at moments to bode ill.

The most significant scene in Part I is the one in which Delano watches Babo shave Don Benito, and the American captain's ideas about black people, which the work as a whole demolishes, flit through his mind. Among other things, he is amused by "an odd instance of the African love of bright colors and fine shows, in the black's informally taking from the flag-locker a great piece of bunting of all hues, and lavishly tucking it under his master's chin for an apron." When Babo chooses the sharpest razor, Don Benito's agitation loosens the bunting that opens up, so that one broad fold sweeps the floor and Delano sees that it is the flag of Spain that

Babo has chosen to drape over Don Benito; but Delano smiles, thinking this reflects the black's love of gay colors. Delano presses Don Benito about unusual aspects of the story he has told; Babo somehow cuts his master; and the conversation is cut short. When soon afterward, Babo appears on deck with a bleeding cheek, Delano concludes that Don Benito has wreaked his anger at having been hurt, and he has his one brief feeling about slavery as an institution, a kind of sentimental regret: "Ah, this slavery breeds ugly passions in man." But when he sees Don Benito leaning on Babo as if nothing had happened, the relationship of master and slave again seems good to him. Moreover, it is a picture of the black man in chains that gives him his final reassurance that all is as it should be. The wind has risen, and acting for the sick Spanish captain, he has brought the *San Dominick* close to his own ship. Delano, whom Don Benito has refused to accompany, is about to leave the cabin to get into the small boat to return across a narrow passage of water. He is frightened, for the giant Atufal seems more a sentry guarding Don Benito, whom Delano now suspects of villainy, than a captive. But when he safely passes Atufal and the "screened sun in the quiet camp of the west" lights the scene, with the reassuring, normal "chained figure of the black," he smiles at the "phantoms" that have mocked him. As he takes leave of Don Benito, whom he now trusts again, and seats himself in his whaleboat, Don Benito suddenly springs over the bulwark to land in the boat and is, Delano thinks, about to murder him as a prelude to seizing his ship. Babo on the rail overhead stands "poised, in the act of leaping, as if with desperate fidelity to befriend his master to the last." Delano flings Don Benito aside in order to tackle Babo, who lands with his dagger pointed at Delano's heart. He grasps the weapon and flings Babo down into the bottom of the boat, which begins to speed away from the *San Dominick*. "At this juncture, the left hand of Captain Delano, on one side, again clutched the half-reclining Don Benito . . . while his right foot, on the other side, ground the prostrate negro." Looking down, Delano sees Babo aiming with a second dagger at the heart of Don Benito, his face expressing "the centred purpose of his soul." Then the mask is, for Delano, torn from the relationship of Don Benito and Babo. It is now clear that the slaves have been in control all along after an earlier revolt; all that Delano has seen has been the play of master and slave, the erstwhile slaves performing their expected roles, the erstwhile master playing his role under Babo's direction. Delano looks back at the ship and sees the blacks "with mask torn away" flourishing hatchets, in what to him is "ferocious piratical revolt." He sees also the canvas ripped away from the prow and the skeleton of Don Alexandro Aranda, the owner of most of the slaves, mounted on the bow as the ship's figurehead, in place of its original emblem. Babo, offering no resistance, is bound and hoisted onto Delano's ship. From this point on, he utters no word. Delano's men board the *San Dominick* where, with superior arms, they overwhelm the blacks, who battle to the last possible moment. Sometime later the whole affair is the subject of investigation by the vice-regal courts in Lima, "City of Kings."

Part II is Don Benito's deposition to the court, which many critics accept as a presentation of the full reality beneath the appearance seen by Delano.[5] But Melville's introduction to it, to the effect that the extracts will, "it is hoped" (299), shed light on the preceding narrative, immediately casts doubt on whether it indeed illuminates the most significant realities. It does, however, set the simple facts straight, making it known that on the seventh day of the *San Dominick*'s voyage the slaves had revolted under the leadership of Babo, killing all the crew except those essential to the running of the ship. They then demanded of Don Benito whether there were any Negro countries nearby to which they might go and, discovering that there were none, ordered that they be taken to Senegal no matter how dangerous or difficult the voyage. Don Benito, pretending to consent, headed for the island of Santa María, presumably for water, but actually in the hope that he would there encounter help. Babo informed Don Benito that he had made up his mind to kill Don Alexandro because the slaves could not otherwise be sure of their liberty, and also as a warning to the others that they would follow him if they played the slaves false. On the fourth day thereafter, at sunrise, the negro Babo showed him the skeleton of Don Alexandro, "which had been substituted for the ship's proper figurehead—the image of Christobal Colon, the discoverer of the New World." Babo asked him whose skeleton it was "and whether, from its whiteness, he should not think it was a white's" (304–5). He then asked the same question of each Spaniard in turn, warning them that they would all go "soul and body" [6] the same way as Don Alexandro if he saw them plotting against the Negroes. When, approaching Santa María for water, the rebels saw Delano's ship in the harbor, they covered the skeleton figurehead, and Babo planned how to hide the true state of affairs, warning Don Benito that if he made any attempt to reveal the facts he would be stabbed. Babo made plans "uniting deceit and defense," including the pretense that the Ashantee hatchet carriers were simply at work polishing hatchets, whereas they were actually preparing to use them if necessary, and the pretense that Atufal was chained, whereas the iron collar was part of his costume and he could remove it at any time. Four elderly blacks were placed on high so that they could keep discipline and give orders when necessary. Don Benito was commanded to tell the story Babo invented for him. The rest was theater, the "play" of master and slave, directed by Babo who, at the same time, acted the part of personal slave to Don Benito, the better to control his performance. *Benito Cereno* is indeed a "juggling play" (282); the roles of master and slave are juggled.

Part III opens: "If the Deposition have served as the key to fit into the lock of the complications which precede it, then, as a vault whose door has been flung back, the *San Dominick*'s hull lies open today" (313). It is an eloquent "If," implying that the deposition is not the key to the reality underlying past events but only to some of the surface perplexities. Part III relates what occurred during and after the voyage to Lima. Delano feels keenly how wrong he was to suspect Don Benito, and Don Benito consoles him. Delano in return tries to console Don Benito, who cannot emerge from the darkness of the voyage: "But the past is passed; why moralize upon it? Forget it. See, yon bright sun has forgotten it all, and the blue sea, and the blue sky; these have turned over new leaves" (314). Don Benito's response is, "Because they have no memory, because they are not human." But the American, who sees only the moment, who has no sense of the influence of the past on both present and future, protests: "You are saved; you are saved: what has cast such a shadow upon you?" Don Benito replies with the most frequently quoted and most misunderstood phrase in the tale: "The negro."

The conclusion again joins Babo and Don Benito:

> Some months after, dragged to the gibbet at the tail of a mule, the black met his voiceless end. The body was burned to ashes; but for many days, the head, that hive of subtlety, fixed on a pole in the Plaza, met, unabashed, the gaze of the whites; and across the Plaza looked towards St. Bartholomew's church, in whose vaults slept then, as now, the recovered bones of Aranda: and across the Rimac bridge looked towards the monastery, on Mount Agonia without; where, three months after being dismissed by the court, Benito Cereno, borne on the bier, did, indeed, follow his leader. (315)

The conclusion does not answer all questions; it gives no final verdict about the men involved. Instead, new questions are suggested. Why does Melville have Babo die "unabashed" while he has Don Benito die at the height of agony? Why does the last sentence end with the idea of following one's leader? And why does the last sentence as a whole leave vague the question of whether Babo or Don Benito died first? Why does Melville show them always together even in death? The gray vapors have not all been blown away. Shadows remain, and no moral judgments have even been hinted—except of slavery.

What lies in the shadows of *Benito Cereno?* Its every page is so rich in implications that the question can never be fully answered, but when one notes fundamental correspondences uniting the artistic methods in the work, and where they point, the main ideas that animate it stand out.

Melville knew that the master-slave relationship does not depend on color, that no race is naturally fit to be either master or slave, that both whites and nonwhites have been slaves at some time in human history: white Oberlus in *The Encantadas* enslaves other whites; Babo reports that Atufal was a king in his country, though he, Babo, was a slave even then. And *Benito Cereno* (as any reader, whatever his other ideas about the work, will agree) refutes ideas like those of Delano that the black person is suited by nature to be the white person's servant and that blacks have innate qualities making them the "indisputable inferiors" of whites.

But Melville knew also that in the Americas, history took a peculiar turn: slavery was given a "racial twist," [7] and minds were twisted in accordance, *black* becoming almost synonymous with *slave* and *white* with *master.* Even those black Americans who became free continued generally to be viewed in the shadow of slavery, as Delano's "humorous" thinking about free men of color illustrates.

Through this story of black slave and white Spanish master and the reversal of the color situation, Melville seeks out the essential form and nature of slavery, which, like the *San Dominick,* shows "no colors." Seemingly paradoxically, he uses color in his probing for what is colorless.

Black and white in *Benito Cereno* designate the dynamic opposites in the master-slave relationship. Within the context of the system in which they operate, they are *inseparable, irreconcilable* and *interchangeable:* the violent potential of their opposition must build up and eventually break out "whoever be the thrall." [8] This is what Melville makes visible.

The inseparability of master and slave is expressed almost entirely by pictorial means. It is the subject of the whole series of tableaux picturing Don Benito and Babo, which unfolds steadily from the moment of their simultaneous entrance into the story to their virtually simultaneous exit: Babo standing, "like a shepherd's dog," beside Don Benito; Babo offering Don Benito a cordial, his arm encircling him; Babo kneeling to adjust Don Benito's shoe buckle, rubbing out a spot on his sleeve, shaving him, curling and costuming him, placing a cushion behind his back, cooling him with a large feather fan, chafing his brow, smoothing his hair, gazing into his eyes, leading him away when he is overcome, refusing to be separated from him, making himself into a sort of crutch for him, and flinging himself into the whaleboat after him, still the faithful servant, as Delano thinks. In all these scenes, which are like photographic stills, master and slave are bound together, their social connection constituting their chain.

The inseparability is what is apparent in a first reading. Rereading reveals that the irreconcilability of master and slave and the violent potential of the relationship are intimated in the same tableaux. The beautiful, peaceful picture of the relationship as Delano sees it is, on second reading, seen to be superimposed upon the picture of master and slave locked in eternal conflict, as in the shaving scene. After Don Benito's leap for freedom, the irreconcilability of master and slave is expressed openly by Babo's knife aimed at Don Benito's heart in the whaleboat; by Don Benito's turning away from Babo at the trial; and by Babo's confrontation of Don Benito across the Plaza and the Rimac bridge, when the two are seen at opposite poles. But they continue to be seen in indivisible relationship.

The most interesting aspect of the master-slave relationship as Melville envisions it in *Benito Cereno* is the interchangeability of master and slave, indicating that the assignment of black to slave position and white to master role is not immutable or natural; the only natural thing is to try to free oneself when enslaved; the only immutable thing is the fundamental nature of slavery itself, with its destruction of both master and slave. The carefully crafted scenes in which Delano reacts to Don Benito and Babo together show Melville intrigued by the switching of roles, and it may be this that drew him to the story. (One is reminded of the "assailants and assailed reversed" in "Donelson" in *Battle-Pieces.*) How craftily he speaks of Babo dressing Don Benito's hair with the hand of a "master"! And with what less obvious art he early finds "something so incongrous in the Spaniard's apparel, as almost to suggest the image of an invalid courtier tottering about London streets in the time of the plague" (251), since, if we stop to think, not only is the idea suggested that Don Benito's costume is incongruous to his present position as slave, but also the reminder that the plague was a disaster for all, mighty as well as humble.

The four basic aspects of the master-slave relationship—the inseparability, the irreconcilability, the interchangeability, and the violent potential of the combination of parts within the system— are presented as if in black-and-white graphic art. Melville's purpose in the use of black and white is most openly hinted when Delano sees the whites and blacks on deck like pieces on a chessboard, for chess is a game in which white and black are essentially equal. The opposing colors merely represent their opposition; either color may find itself in the better or worse position. The chessboard may be turned around, and black may stand where white has been. But the game itself remains the same, and warfare is its essence. So it is with the black and white men of the *San Dominick*. The positions of black and white may change, but so long as the men are on board the ship of masters and slaves, warfare is inevitable.

This chess image indicates the use Melville makes of black and white throughout. It can best be described in terms of the negative and positive images in black-and-white photography. Melville's technique is to present one image while suggesting the other. In the "positive" and "negative" what is black in one is white in the other, but the basic picture remains the same. In the series of tableaux in which Don Benito and Babo appear, always joined, always opposed, one figure is black and one is white. But their positions, as compared with the ones they occupied before the revolt, have been exchanged; black is now master, white is enslaved. Delano does not know this, so what he sees is what is "normal" to him as a man of the Americas, that is, the "positive" image in which white is master, black is slave. But the reader—or rather the rereader—knows that the "negative" is really accurate here and that the slave figure now has a white face and the master figure's face is black. Were Delano to see the "negatives," the black figure being shaved by the white one, the white figure kneeling before the black one and looking up at him, the white wearing nothing but coarse patched trousers, the black in elegant costume, he would think of the ugliness, not the beauty, of the relationship.

Could the contrast in dress "denoting their relative positions" be eliminated and the figures show "no colors," one would see the form and nature of the relationship without being influenced by social custom. Through the mocking question that Melville has Babo ask, not once but of each Spaniard in succession, about whether from the whiteness of Don Alexandro's skeleton he could not conclude that it was a white man's, he almost openly tells us to look beneath the skin colors in each positive and negative to the x-ray-like picture of slavery-in-essence. If we follow his clue, then beneath each tableau and its opposite we see two skeletons differentiated only in that one stands in the position of master and one in the position of slave. Power, signified by the razor in the shaving scene, may change hands; Melville again hints this when, in the deposition, a Spanish sailor holds a razor seized from the pocket of his own jacket now worn by a "shackled" black and the reader sees him "aiming it at the negro's throat." But whoever at any moment is in power, violence—past, present, and future—is implicit in the relationship. The skeleton of Aranda symbolizes the nature of such a ship as the *San Dominick,* which must of necessity have "death for the figurehead." The skeleton is a great imaginative creation exactly suited to the essential reality Melville prods each reader to arrive at in his own mind.

Beneath the surface of *Benito Cereno* is also its own skeletal structure. Although on first reading the development of the work seems linear, moving from the 1799 present back to the past revolt and forward to events subsequent to the quelling of the revolt, once *Benito Cereno* is reread, it demands to be seen as one triangular form in which the Spaniard, the North American, and the black slave are seen in a historical interrelationship, each representing a point of view, not inborn, but the result of his experience in the Americas in his time.

The first part of the work focuses on the view from Delano's angle. It might be entitled "Delano's Misconceptions," including, in addition to those he forms on the *San Dominick,* those mistaken preconceptions he brings on board with him. The latter are primary. Only because of his failure to see them as fully human beings can the blacks play their deception upon him. Even in the moments when they chafe at playing their role and their masks slip, Delano's notion that serving whites is the natural role of blacks is so fixed that his doubts are stilled; for example, when they act in defense, closing in behind him, he thinks they are acting in deference, "a Kaffir guard of honor." For he has been conditioned to think of blacks, slave or free, as fitted for servitude; that idea is what justifies slavery to him and hence makes it possible for him to see beauty in the Don Benito-Babo relationship. Though he is not himself a slaveowner, he shares the master mentality in regard to the nature and purpose of black people. They are to him at first like delightful animals and then, when the battle is out in the

open, like wild beasts; at no time are they men and women. It is
important to note, in connection with the triangular structure of
the work, that the animal imagery, for which Melville has been
criticized, is strictly limited to Part I, which centers on Delano's
way of seeing. What Melville has given Delano is the outlook of the
average white eighteenth-century American to whom slavery and
the slave trade were accepted institutions. That Delano comes
from New England (from Duxbury, close to Boston) rather than
from the southern states does not make his outlook different from
that of the average white American of his day. Many a respected
New England fortune was made directly in the slave trade or in the
"triangular" voyages that set out from Boston with cargo to be
exchanged for slaves in Africa; these slaves, if they survived the
middle passage, were exchanged for sugar and molasses in the
West Indies, and the molasses was then sold in New England for
the manufacture of rum. Moral Christian New Englanders managed to justify slavery by thinking of blacks as inferior by nature.
The *Encyclopedia Americana* says of the New England fortunes
founded on the slave trade that this was wealth to which "no
odium attached in the politest and most moral circles until toward
the end of the eighteenth century."

Delano is a man who does not like to dwell upon unpleasant
things or puzzle himself about complicated truths. It is he and not
Melville who sees things on the *San Dominick* in black-and-white
simplicity. Closing his eyes to all hints of complex and unhappy
things, he is like one who, "feeling incipient seasickness," strives
"by ignoring the symptoms, to get rid of the malady" (271). This is
his attitude to the end: "But the past is passed; why moralize upon
it?" Like the average American of Melville's day who was also
striving, by ignoring the symptoms to avoid the malady, Delano
has dismissed from his mind the brief thought that slavery might
be the basis for all that has happened on the *San Dominick,* and
he will not "moralize" enough about the past to return to that
thought and apply it to his own country.

Melville's ironical treatment of Delano's preconceptions and
wishful thinking conveys much of the underlying reality of the
situation on the *San Dominick* and all that it represents. The simple
ironies are easy to perceive. They involve mainly those things that

Delano sees in one way and that later turn out to be the opposite: the "docility," the "contentment," the "unsophisticated nature," and the "limited minds" of the blacks. But there is in *Benito Cereno* a duplex irony, exquisitely worked and elaborately hidden. A few examples will illustrate Melville's peculiar method here.

Delano is impressed by the closeness of Don Benito and Babo. Factually they are physically close, mentally hemispheres apart. Below the fact and the simple irony are the realities: the reciprocal enchainment of master and slave; the explosion that must come from their being locked together in the prison of slavery; and the death sentence for master as well as for slave. They are close, but in a way that Delano cannot understand.

Another example involves Delano's amusement at Babo's enjoyment as he uses the Spanish flag as an apron. Delano thinks his use of the flag reflects Babo's love of bright colors. On the factual level it is true that Babo enjoys using the flag, but false that it is because of a love of bright colors. On the level of deeper reality, his enjoyment of the use of the flag as a rag and his draping of the captain of the slave transportation ship in the standard of slavery-sponsoring Spain have historical implications that are lost on Delano who, in contrast to Melville and Babo, is "incapable of satire and irony" (257) and incapable of understanding it.

A third example goes to the heart of the tale. "Ah," Delano thinks on seeing the cut on Babo's cheek, "this slavery breeds ugly passions in man." Although he quickly dismisses the thought when he sees master and slave together again as if nothing has happened, the meaning of the *San Dominick* experience is precisely that the master-slave relationship creates the violent passions. Delano cannot see that ugliness is the nature of the relationship, a direct opposite of the beauty he persists in seeing when he decides the shedding of blood is just part of a "love quarrel." The irony lies in Delano's not seeing the meaning of what he himself has said.

Don Benito stands at the next vertex of the triangle. His membership in "one of the most enterprising and extensive mercantile families in all those provinces" along the Spanish Main (258); his friendship from youth with Don Alexandro, owner of so large a group of slaves; his position as captain—all place him firmly in the ruling group in the South American world. To assume that Melville intended him to represent goodness is to assume that he brings these things into the tale for no reason at all and takes lightly the fact that Cereno is captain of a ship that transports slaves, a role he views with horror everywhere else in his writings; in *Clarel* captains who transported slaves, though they did not do the actual enslaving, are described as guilty of one of the worst "sins refined, crimes of the spirit" and "These, chiefly these, to doom submit" (Pt. II, Canto xxxvi).

The critical interpretation that Don Benito represents goodness is sometimes justified by references to his devout Christianity, evidenced by the crucifix on the bulwark of his cabin, the thumbed missal on the table, and his retreat to a monastery. But the evidences of Don Benito's Christianity only highlight the irony of his connection with slaveowning, since Christian values are contradicted by his role. For Melville's general attitude toward Don Benito's kind of piety, we need only refer to any other Melville work in which slavery or oppression are under consideration. One in particular is pertinent in regard to Don Benito—the reference in *Mardi* to the master who may shrive his soul, take every sacrament, give up the ghost on bended knee, and who yet is destined to die despairing. Since this is the very fate that Melville assigns to Don Benito, the earlier passage takes on special significance, as does the later passage in the "Supplement" to *Battle-Pieces*, which speaks of slavery as "an atheistical iniquity."

Don Benito represents no abstract moral quality, good or bad; he is presented as a man imprisoned in a specific social and historical context, a man who has inherited the role of master which must destroy him unless he is able to free himself by freeing the slave. ("The slave there carries the padlock, but master here carries the key," says Babo [256]). History has presented him, "among South Americans of his class" (251), with the black slave taken from Africa, who acts, when the possibility arises, to free himself, as does Don Benito in his turn.

But what does Melville mean when, in answer to Delano's question about what has cast such a shadow upon him, he has Don Benito reply, "The negro"? Yvor Winters presents an example of the classical response: "His reply in Spanish would have signified not only the negro, or the black man, but by metaphorical extension the basic evil in human nature. The morality of slavery is not an issue in this story; the issue is this, that through a series of acts of performance and of negligence, the fundamental evil of a group of men, evil which normally should have been kept in abeyance, was freed to act. The story is a portrait of that evil in action, as shown in the negroes, and of the effect of the action, as shown in Cereno." If Melville does not intend this, what does he mean to convey?

At the time Don Benito says these words, he is a man haunted by his experience. He does not understand it, but he has some realization that it is linked to his role as master of a ship transporting black slaves "amongst other valuable freight." (Since there seems to be no other reason for Delano to speak at the end of the "trades" and for Cereno to reply that they are only wafting him to his tomb, I take the reference to be Melville's pun in connection with the "business" in which the ship was engaged.) Cereno knows his fate has been inseparable from Babo's. The Negro's mind is unknown to him, but he has gone through an experience akin to slavery, and he has a gnawing sense of the slave's condition. He cannot follow Delano's advice to forget the past. Even in the monastery he cannot find sanctuary from it. Like the master in *Mardi*, though he perform every religious rite, he is doomed to die despairing.

When Don Benito answers "The negro" to explain what has cast the great shadow upon him, it is Melville's two-word summary of what he has been developing all along: that while the master-slave relationship exists, neither slave nor master is free of the other. *Each lives in the shadow of the other.* The shadow hanging over Don Benito is imaginatively related to the slavery that "puts out the sun at noon" in *Mardi*, the noon that is like dusk in *Benito Cereno* (272) and the "screened sun" that Delano finds reassuring.

The last part of *Benito Cereno* focuses attention on the fact that whereas the view from the angle of the white North American and of the white Spaniard in South America have been presented, the view from the angle of the third member of the triangle, Babo, the enslaved black man from Africa, remains missing to the end. But Melville does not leave the reader without clues to his thinking, although he presents the tale (as a white sailor presents a knot to the American) as a thing "for someone else to undo."

What do we know of Babo from *Benito Cereno*? His blackness

marks him as the man taken by force from Africa to be a slave in
the Americas. He has a rich intelligence: he has the qualities of
mind of a master psychologist, strategist, general, playwright, im-
presario, and poet. Melville endows him with his own poetic
insight into the symbolic implications that can be found in significant figures and objects: the skeleton, the black giant who may
throw off his chains and will not ask pardon, the padlock and key,
the Spanish flag used as a rag. We know that Babo has a strong
sense of his blackness and an intense resentment of the whites'
attitude of superiority, as well as an appreciation of its humor.

We can know, also, that Babo does not act out of innate evil and
without motive. Babo's purpose, and that of the other blacks, is a
fact clearly stated in Don Benito's deposition to the court. It is to
get the black slave group, which fears reenslavement, to a "negro
country." The killing of Don Alexandro has a twofold purpose: to
ensure the group's newly won freedom and to warn the other
whites. Not even Babo's assault on Don Benito in the whaleboat is
an expression of pure hatred. The brief but brilliant scene is a
reminder of the one in *White-Jacket* in which White-Jacket, swing-
ing to the "instinct" in all living beings, tries to murder Captain
Claret, wanting to haul him from an earthly to a heavenly tribunal
to decide between him and his oppressor. The justice meted out at
the end of *Benito Cereno* is also earthly justice. Specifically, it is the
justice of the white European "Christian" colonizers and "civi-
lizers" as determined by the slavery-sanctioning courts acting for
the Spanish king in the "City of Kings." There is reason why the
head of Babo, fixed on a pole in the Plaza in Lima, can meet
"unabashed" the gaze of the whites; their justice is not his justice,
their good and evil are not his good and evil; slaveowner and slave
do not have the same definition of justice any more than of liberty;
what is just and right to the slaveowner is slavery; what is just and
right to the slave is freedom. And, Melville implies further, the
slaveowner has a double standard of justice. What is criminal
when done by the slave is right and just when he himself does it.
Babo's actions are considered atrocities by the whites, but the
manner of *his* death, dragged alive to the gibbet at the tail of a
mule, constitutes justice to them. Don Alexandro's skeleton on the
prow proves the slaves barbaric, but Babo's head on a pole in the

Plaza is civilized. The enslavement of Don Benito is evil; the enslavement of the blacks is taken for granted. The description of
Babo's end, which makes more than questionable the justice of the
civilized white Christian rulers in Lima, is Melville's way of dra-
matizing the ideas presented more journalistically in the *Typee* passage about readers in the colonizing countries who are horrified by
the acts of the "diabolical heathens" against the invaders of their
lands, but view with equanimity the atrocities committed by their
own representatives, and call upon all Christendom to applaud
their courage and their justice. In *Benito Cereno* Melville gives his
reader an opportunity to test her or his own standard of justice:
Will the atrocities inflicted on Babo (and on the shackled blacks by
the white sailors) horrify the reader as much as the atrocities inflicted on Don Alexandro and the other whites, killed during and
after the revolt against enslavement? Will the reader be aware of
the original atrocity, slavery, which gives rise to all the rest? Or
will he miss what Melville is saying because he, too, takes the
double standard for granted?

So neither Babo nor blackness stands for Evil in this extraordinary work. Indeed, it would have been strange if Melville, in whose
work as a whole there is such a large cast of black characters of all
kinds, had chosen here to make blackness the sign of any inherent
quality. Far from presenting Babo as a clear-cut moral symbol,
Melville presents him as a mystery that cannot be easily unraveled
and that is not fully explained even at the end of the book, though
hints have been given to the reader. "Since I cannot do deeds, I
will not speak words," Melville imagines his silence after his capture to say, the likely implication being that Babo feels the only
language the whites will understand is action. The slave, Melville
seems to be telling America, has yet to be heard from; it would be
well to imagine his condition and what is in his mind.

Just as Babo does not represent Evil, changeless and causeless, so
Benito Cereno is not a fable carrying the moral that the good are
powerless unless they recognize that there is Evil in humanity. The
evil that the work implies one should recognize is specific and
meaningful—the slavery that was introduced into the Western
Hemisphere on the heels of its "discovery" by Columbus acting for
Spain. To Melville, once widely traveled sailor, South America

and North America were closely related. So were slave revolts and wars arising from slavery; the section on the extreme south of Vivenza in *Mardi* foresees violence in the form of both slave uprising and war between North and South, and in *Battle-Pieces* John Brown, whose aim was to touch off a slave insurrection throughout the South, is the heavenly portent of the war. The ship that had carried the figurehead of Columbus conveys three things closely related in Melville's imagination: slavery; Spain in the "New World"; and the United States, once thought of as Columbia. Melville saw Spain as America's predecessor, in that sense her leader, in the hemisphere, and he felt her ultimate fate there, as signified by the *San Dominick's,* to be a portent for his own country.

At the time of the *San Dominick* events, 1799, Spain was still a great colonial power in whose dominions in South America (awarded to her by a Spanish-born pope), slavery was still firmly planted. But, as the Cuban poet Nicolás Guillén suggests, it was also a time in South America that was so seething with rebellion that only the blind or deaf could fail to perceive the signs or hear the subterranean roar or feel the tremors. Just a few years later independence and emancipation were proclaimed by the South American revolutionaries. By 1825 all the Spanish colonies on the South American continent were free. And by the time *Benito Cereno* was written, the claws of the old Spanish lion had almost all been pulled: the power of Spain in the Americas was over, only Cuba and Puerto Rico remaining to her. Melville was able to look back and see the year 1799 as a time when the sun of Spain was already beginning to set and when the empire that had begun with Columbus's discoveries three hundred years before would soon be no more.

The indications that Melville had the example of Spain in mind in *Benito Cereno* are many. The *San Dominick* bears as its "principal relic of faded grandeur" the sternpiece carved with the arms of Castile and León. The Spanish flag is what Babo chooses to place under Don Benito's chin in the shaving scene, to catch hairs and to trail on the floor. At the end of the shaving scene, the flag is "tumbled up, and tossed back into the flag-locker." The other Spanish symbol the blacks remove from sight is the figurehead of Columbus, symbol for Spain of its expansion and for the blacks of their enslavement. The substitution of the skeleton of the slaveowner is emblematic for Melville of the doom of Spain and of death coming, because of slavery, to the United States. (The ship in Amasa Delano's narrative has no mention of a figurehead or of a skeleton.) The name of the *San Dominick* (selected instead of the name in the original account) also emphasizes the association of the ship with Spain, whose rapid conquest and colonization of the New World began with San Domingo in 1494. The island, originally called Isla Española by Columbus and later Santo Domingo or San Domingo, was the center of Spanish control in the Western Hemisphere.

There are at least a half dozen passages in *Benito Cereno* that hint that the connection should be made between the Spanish experience and the American one. In a work in which no word is wasted, in which almost every descriptive sentence contains a glimmer of deeper meaning, these brief passages should be given their full value. One is the single-sentence paragraph that shows the two ships, the Spanish and the American, anchored together (291). Another is Delano's mental association of Spaniards with the "good folks of Duxbury, Massachusetts," although, as ever, he is unaware of the deeper implications of his thought. A related idea is suggested by mention of the Cereno family as a "mercantile" one with business dealings in all the provinces along the coast; Melville thus makes it a parallel of the equally enterprising and extensive mercantile families of early New England in their relations with the South (families that also had members who were captains of merchant ships that transported slaves and profited from slavery and were on good terms with slaveholders like Don Alexandro). The picture of Don Benito, Babo, and Delano in their last moments together on the *San Dominick* highlights slavery as that which links the Spaniard and the American in a kind of alliance. Babo stands in the middle: "And so still presenting himself as a crutch, and walking between the two captains, he advanced with them towards the gangway; while still, as if full of kindly contrition, Don Benito would not let go the hand of Captain Delano, *but retained it in his, across the black's body*" (293; my emphasis). Tearing his hand loose, the Spanish captain says to the American, "Go, and God guard you better than me." In the light of what Melville says about the United States and slavery in his other works, this prayer can be understood not only as that of the captain who represents Spain for the captain who represents America but also as that of Melville for his own country. In the whaleboat there is a last view of the three together, and here Delano holds the center of the stage: with his left hand he clutches Don Benito; with his right foot he holds down "the prostrate negro"—a fascinating enactment and reminder of the scene depicted on the sternpiece of the Spanish ship at the beginning of the story, even echoing the words "prostrate" and "writhing." In this enactment, the masks are off, and it is Delano, representing America, who has his foot on the prostrate slave. What land, then, has Melville had in mind all along? Remember that Delano is the first and last in the story to read the words "Follow your leader" on the side of the ship. Finally, there is the ship's flawed bell that Delano hears in the *San Dominick*'s narrow corridor, a bell mentioned twice earlier in the tale: "It was the echo of the ship's flawed bell, *striking the hour,* drearily reverberated in this subterranean vault" (my emphasis). Delano's mind is responsive for a moment to the "portent," but the sight of his own American ship "lying peacefully at anchor . . . rising and falling on the short waves by the *San Dominick*'s side" (292) calms him, and he forgets the echo that portends more than the imminent crisis on the ship. The image of the flawed bell suggests the Liberty Bell, flawed, like the *San Dominick*'s, in two ways, the actual crack signifying to Melville the spiritual flaw. Writing of a Spanish ship in the Americas, Melville is thinking of the United States with its tragic flaw. But Delano does not see the portent for the United States of 1799 that was also, seemingly, "lying peacefully at anchor." He is too much a white man of his time to learn much of value from the *San Dominick* experience. The reader, however, can see truths Delano might have seen had he been better able to understand the past. For one thing, Delano might have recognized that the past, present, and future are a continuum, as Melville says in a short paragraph when Babo leaps over the bulwalks: "All this, with what preceded and what followed, occurred with such involutions of rapidity, that past, present, and future seemed one" (294). But to Delano the realization of historical connections is as fleeting as the action. When he tells Don Benito later that it is useless to moralize about the past, he is the typical white American of his time closing his eyes to the catastrophe history is demonstrating will come if slavery continues. Were his eyes open, he would see that all on the surface of a society, as of a ship, may wear an ordinary, even a calm and peaceful aspect, and yet be soon to erupt.

By the time of *Benito Cereno* Melville's artistic methods had moved far from the almost straightforward expression of ideas that characterizes *Mardi*'s section on slavery in Vivenza. His way in *Benito Cereno* is like that of an artist carving a three-dimensional scene in ivory and ebony, working subtle designs that are hidden away in the recesses. Still, the ideas in the tale are not meant to be hidden forever. The clues are there. But preconceptions about black and white, as in the case of Delano, have led to misunderstanding and even to literal misreading. One example of the latter is especially interesting. It reports that Atufal has been appearing before Don Benito periodically to ask his pardon,[9] whereas the plain fact is that Atufal repeatedly refuses to ask pardon. Now, Atufal's appearances and refusals are important to the whole interpretation of the story. The purpose of the scenes—for both Babo and Melville—is twofold. On a "plot" level it is to provide Babo, whose muscular strength is slight, with an aide of great physical might who, since he is apparently chained, will not be feared but will be able to throw off his chains and overpower the American should that become necessary. The poetic purpose is of more profound importance. In Atufal, Babo—like Melville—has a symbol of the enslaved black in revolt, whose powers and will to freedom have been underestimated, a giant who can throw off his chains and, unabashed, will not ask for pardon. That Melville shares with Babo, in the Atufal scenes and elsewhere, his own kind of poetic imagination, his own way of seeing the implications beneath the surface of a situation, and his own way of creating a scene on different levels is the best single clue to Melville's intentions. He is doing in this tale what he has Babo do, create a work of great imagination with a surface appearance and a hidden reality. He would not have made Babo a playwright and poet so like himself in his choice of symbols—above all, the skeleton symbol—had he wanted to portray him as a naturally destructive force. Instead, he depicts a Babo with natural creative gifts who is made destructive by the historical "condition" of black slavery in the Americas, a condition of which Melville speaks indirectly through Don Benito's consolation to Delano: "So far may even the best man err, in judging the conduct of one with the recesses of whose condition he is not acquainted" (314). Of course Melville's purpose is more encompassing than Babo's; he is opposed to slavery whether white or black is enslaved.

Free of preoccupation with black as a symbol of evil and with good and evil as mystic abstractions unrelated to "place and time," [10] the reader can perceive the inner reality of *Benito Cereno* and can hear the undertone echoing in the "subterranean vault" of the *San Dominick* as it forewarns the United States of a tragic fate to result from its tragic flaw. Penetrating the surface account given by Amasa Delano, Melville saw the "haunted pirate ship" of slavery with "its skeleton gleaming in the horizontal moonlight . . . casting a gigantic ribbed shadow upon the water" (272, 298).

Notes

1. References are to text in *Great Short Works of Herman Melville,* ed. Warner Berthoff (New York: Harper & Row, 1970).
2. For text see *Benito Cereno,* ed. John P. Runden (Boston: Heath, 1965). The Yvor Winters passage later quoted also appears in this edition. So does one of the outstanding dissenting views, "The Enduring Innocence of Captain Amasa Delano," by Allen Guttmann.
3. See *Mardi* (Ch. clxii); "The Swamp Angel" in which the black angel, in the form of the great Parrott gun, is God's messenger bombarding Charleston; and *Clarel* (Pt. II, Canto xxxvi). The quoted words are from "The Apparition" in *Battle-Pieces.*
4. In *Israel Potter* it is necessary to "pierce" the haze masking the inner reality of the battle of the *Bonhomme Richard* and the *Serapis.*
5. Warner Berthoff in his introduction to the story says the court documents "unravel its riddling mysteries."
6. The word *soul* appears twice and only in connection with Babo.
7. Eric Williams, *Capitalism and Slavery* (London: Andre Deutsch, 1964), p. 7.
8. *Mardi,* Ch. clxii.
9. Richard Chase, *Herman Melville* (New York: Macmillan, 1949), p. 158.
10. From "The Slain Collegians" in *Battle-Pieces.*

7.

The "History" of the Indian-hater in Its Context, *The Confidence-Man:* Grotesque Art for Melville's Ideas of the War on the American Indian

Although designed as a puzzle never to be completely solved, *The Confidence-Man: His Masquerade* (1857) [1] makes one thing indisputable: that by the time of its composition Melville had no faith that the United States would voluntarily see its ills and dangers. In his bitter state of mind in 1855–56 [2] he looked at the "time and place" to which, in the first chapter, the Christ-suggesting figure and his writings seem "somehow inappropriate" and found what he saw to be hideous: lust—for money, for land, for a sense of power to gull others—had brought slavery, poverty, wars of expansion, the near extermination of the native "Indian" population, and was now leading to some great total disaster. As a result, and as if following the advice and example of Hamlet (who appears in a parenthesis that has the force of italics), he undertook to show "the very age and body of the time his form and pressure"; plotted to catch conscience by means of a play; and, in the spirit of Hamlet assaulting his mother, set up a glass before the country that would confront it with so repulsive a reflection of itself as to cause self-revulsion, make it repent the past, and "avoid what is to come." He seems from the concluding line of the work to have retained one grain of hopeless hope: "Something further may follow of this Masquerade"—the masque he had presented.

111

To give vent to his extreme feeling and to shock his readers into self-knowledge, he needed an extreme form of expression. Responding to that demand, his imagination created a unique variation of the grotesque, a language new in American literature. In structure, imagery, diction, in the conception of characters, situations, and dialogues, and in the narratives told along the way—above all in the much-misread story of the Indian-hater—the art of *The Confidence-Man* reflects the grotesque reality that Melville saw beneath the nation's masks.

In his nightmare vision, America assumes the shape of a Mississippi River steamboat, the *Fidèle,* hurrying downstream on a day of diabolical jokes toward and then past Cairo, the last place where there is still a chance to turn from the downriver course. The passengers, representing the nationalities and sections of the country, distrust each other but do not wonder about the state of the *Fidèle.* On this "ship of fools" (iii, 22) where each has his own self-deception, the shared delusion is that the ship is sound. "Speeds the daedal boat as a dream" (xvi, 105) on an April Fools' Day when all is chaos and values are "topsy-turvy."

The Confidence-Man is a jigsaw puzzle, demanding the putting together of countless descriptions, disguises, encounters, narratives, images, names, phrases, and other odd bits and pieces to form an overall picture. But even when most of the pieces are joined, the picture that comes together is and must ever remain partly mysterious, because its central figure, the confidence-man in his many roles, is never allowed to be clearly defined: the puzzle is intended to continue to work in the reader's mind, like the crippled "sol dier's" powder in "the Happy Man" (xviii, 131). But the setting in which the central figure appears is sharply drawn, and this setting is the real subject of the work. The *function* of the confidence-man is almost openly explained in the fragment that is the key piece in the assembling of the jigsaw puzzle. He is the one whom Melville, under the pretense of denying it, conceives as a true "original character" in fiction, the one who "essentially . . . is like a revolving Drummond light, raying away from itself all round it—everything is lit by it, everything starts up to it" (xliv, 330). Whatever his true character, "if any" (xli, 311) the confidence-man serves to test the true characters of the others. He casts his light on a confidence-man society.

Conflicts among people characterize such a society. Manhunting is inherent to it; love cannot exist in it. The picture developed in *The Confidence-Man* is of a masked war: the *Fidèle* resembles a "whitewashed fort"; antagonism among the passengers is featured in every scene and has its echo in the warring impulses within individuals. The *Fidèle,* conglomerating all kinds of misplaced or pretended faith, carrying creatures of prey and victims, is a representation of a psychologically, morally, intellectually sick society, destructive and self-destructive.

No wonder, then, that *The Confidence-Man* is filled with images of disease, alienation and self-alienation, decay, and death. No wonder the cast is composed of grotesquely conceived characters like the old miser whose head looks as if it has been whittled by an idiot out of a knot, who lies close to death but clings to "life and lucre," attracting to him flies lured by the coming of decay, his mind, too, all but moldered away; or like Goneril of cactuslike appearance who hates her husband and—going Shakespeare's Goneril one better—is jealous of her child; or like Moredock, the Indian-hater, who, even late in life, likes to go out for "a few days' shooting at human beings" (xxvii, 219); or like the misanthropic Missourian who, finding them the only ones who serve him well, considers machines the only true Christians and rejoices that the day is at hand when "prompted to it by law," he will shoulder his gun and "go out a boy-shooting" (xxii, 162); or like any one of the other symbolic cripples, invalids, and victims of obsessions of all kinds who people the work. No wonder the lamp of Christianity stinks at the end and the confidence-man blows it out as he leads the old man away to an unknown fate. In this critical time Melville's imagination had to work with such images. The mask of comedy that the work wears has a death's-head grin.

The macabre comedy begins at sunrise with the appearance on deck of a white lamblike figure, "in the extremest sense of the word, a stranger"; the carnival continues through the confidence-man's (and others') disguises; and it ends with him in his synthesized role as "the cosmopolitan," leading an old man out of the cabin while the others in it "who wanted to sleep, not see" lie dead to the world. In each of the confidence-man's appearances, Melville casts doubt on whether he is what he appears to be: the lamblike figure may be an "impostor"; Black Guinea, the beggar, may be a "white operator in disguise"; the cosmopolitan may be intending harm to the old man or saving him from the fate of those in the cabin; in every encounter Melville makes it impossible to define the boundary between the words that express the confidence-man's real thoughts and those that "start up" the one to whom he is speaking.

Among the motley collection of hypocrites, man haters, and fools whom the confidence-man encounters, two pretenders are of particular significance in connection with the chapters on the Indian-hater. The first is a wealthy gentleman with gold sleeve buttons who has a very "winsome" aspect (vii, 50–53); the adjective will become his companion-character's name. He wears a white kid glove on one hand, while the other hand, ungloved, is hardly less white. Melville marvels that hands can retain such spotlessness on the soot-streaked deck of the *Fidèle*. But the explanation is simple: the man avoids touching anything himself; he has a servant to do his touching for him, a man "having to do with dirt on his account." But if, says Melville, "with the same undefiledness of consequences to himself, a gentleman could also sin by deputy, how shocking that would be!" Then he adds: "But it is not permitted to be; and even if it were, no judicious moralist would make proclamation of it." The second character, linked to this one through the idea of sinning by deputy, is Mark Winsome (xxxvi–xxxvii, 265–80). He is a New England mystic philosopher, a caricature of Emerson, who sits "purely and coldly radiant as a prism," who seldom cares to be consistent, and who keeps his love of things "in the lasting condition of an untried abstraction." He, too, has a deputy who acts for him—Egbert, his "practical disciple" who reduces the principles of Mark Winsome to practice, a thriving young merchant, "a practical poet in the West India trade" who looks as if "he might, with the characteristic knack of a true New-Englander, turn even so profitless a thing [as mysticism] to some profitable account." So Mark Winsome, also, is one who has his ideas and questionable desires put into practice by another. The idea of acting by deputy serves as the main link between the sections featuring Winsome and the man with the winsome aspect and the section on Indian-killing.

The account of Moredock the Indian-hater, with its preface on the "metaphysics" of Indian-hating, is told to the cosmopolitan by an Alabamian, Charles Arnold Noble, who recounts almost verbatim what was told time after time by his father's friend, Judge Hall. On the surface this section of the book tells the history of the Indian-killer's war on the Indians as the judge has long "impressed" it on people's minds. Hidden in it (though really not too deeply) is Melville's own view. In his black humor in this section is implied the contrast between what he felt was the true history of the war on the Indian and the mask of "history" he has the judge blandly place over it.

Whatever the judge impresses on his hearers, the Indian in this section is not what the all but unanimous opinion in the critical literature about this story would have him—Melville's symbol of Evil.³ How can one disregard the contrast between the outrageous things Melville has the judge say, in a sequence of increasingly unrestrained remarks, and the matter-of-fact way in which Melville has him say them? To ignore Melville's extravagant caricature of the way American history is told and to fail to sense his anger at what that history has actually been is equivalent to reading Swift's "A Modest Proposal" without awareness of the contrast between its recommendation that the nourishment of the infants of the Irish poor be subsidized so that they might be sold as food for the English landlords and the matter-of-fact way in which that idea is put forward—equivalent to ignoring Swift's bitter attack on the history of English-Irish relations. To establish that Melville's Indian-hating section is, like Swift's essay, a masterpiece of grotesque art to expose the real history of a conquering people and a conquered one is the objective of the remainder of this chapter.

The story of the Indian-killer is told to the cosmopolitan by the one character in the book who is clearly false from the start (xxv, 196–97). Noble's clothes, which are finer than his features, his florid cordiality, the "fictitious" way his vest flushes his cheek, even his "too good to be true" false teeth are instant clues to his spuriousness; the reader must look beneath the mask of his words. It might be said of him, as Melville has him say of Polonius, that he is paralytic all down one side, and that the side of nobleness. (Melville's punning on Noble's name is frequent.) The story that he relates is all rumor, repetition, and rhetoric. This is, or should

be, obvious from the moment Noble, responding to the cosmopolitan's request for a little "history" of Moredock the Indian-hater,
says: "Well: though, as you may gather, I never fully saw the man,
yet, have I, one way and another, heard about as much of him as
any other; in particular, have I heard his history again and again
from my father's friend, James Hall, the judge, you know. In every
company being called upon to give this history, which none could
better do, the judge at last fell into a style so methodic, you would
have thought he spoke less to mere auditors than to an invisible
amanuensis; seemed talking for the press; very impressive way with
him indeed. And I, having an equally impressible memory, think
that, upon a pinch, I can render you the judge upon the colonel
almost word for word" (201).

It is significant that the story has already been three times called
not a story but a "history," and the narration, when it begins, will
associate it with other historical annals and records. The other
narratives told in the course of *The Confidence-Man* are all referred to
as stories; the biography of Moredock is introduced and then
quickly underlined as a history methodically presented by one who
judges what is to be impressed on impressible minds. It is history as
adjudged by writers like Parkman, whose treatment of the Indians
Melville strongly criticized,[4] or like James Hall, whose works
Melville took off from.[5]

The account by Melville's Judge Hall pretends to be judicious.
Some of his statements, taken out of their context, might seem to
be examples of a balanced view. Many of the general attacks
against the Indians, which he circulates, are put forward as examples of what others say. But these seemingly objective statements
are promptly counteracted (by his very next words in some cases),
and other generalizations about Indian evil are openly his own.
Certainly his overall verdict is indisputably on the side of the Indian-killer. The "history" of Moredock the Indian-hater with its
long introduction is Melville's demonstration of the fact that in the
bulk of the recorded history of America's drive to the West, the
Indian has not been judged like the white man whose crimes, as in
this story, are rationalized and even revered. Noble's introductory
remarks to the Judge's story convey Melville's warning that the
"methodic" repetitions of a "history" to impress it upon impressi-

ble minds and the unquestioning verbatim circulation of it by others have made general knowledge of the true relation between the white man and the Indian impossible.

Even before his introductory comments, Noble's preamble to the Moredock story implies a fundamental question: Did this legendary pioneer figure ever really exist? Someone named Moredock probably did. But is the one of the judge's "history" real or legendary? Noble's preface tells of his own attempt once to see the famous Moredock. When he was a boy on a journey west with his father, they came to a cabin whose owner, proudly pointing to a rifle as Moredock's, said the famous Indian-killer was asleep and could not be disturbed, "for the Colonel had been out all night hunting (Indians, mind), and it would be cruel to disturb his sleep." The boy Noble later managed to slip back to the cabin to look around the loft for Moredock; he could see nothing but a pile of wolfskins, a bundle of something like a drift of leaves, and a moss-ball: "That bit of woodland scene was all I saw. No Colonel Moredock there, unless that moss-ball was his curly head, seen in the back view."

Thus Melville hints that the Moredock of the story, when put to the test, has no real substance: "No Colonel Moredock there." He is the stuff of myth and fable. The supposedly material basis for him, in the "back view" that history takes, turns out to be a moss-ball (a growth whose substance accumulates with the passage of time) or a pile of leaves built up by the wind. He is the imaginary "extension" of a society served by Indian-killers, a figure made heroic by that society to justify the hate it feels for those it has wronged, the legendary figure to whom it can transfer its guilt and whose conduct it can then proceed to whitewash. It is in this respect, especially, that the Moredock section of *The Confidence-Man* meshes with the description of the man with the spotless hands and the account of the mystic philosopher who remains aloof and pure while his disciple acts for him. In the Moredock section the society sins by deputy, though no "judicious moralist" (like Judge Hall) "would make proclamation of it."

The last of Noble's prefatory remarks is a quotation from the judge: "For you must know that Indian-hating was no monopoly of Colonel Moredock's but a passion, in one form or another, and to a degree, greater or less, largely shared among the class to which he belonged. And Indian-hating still exists; and, no doubt, will continue to exist, so long as Indians do. Indian-hating, then, shall be my first theme, and Colonel Moredock, the Indian-hater, my next and last." We will return to this at the end of this chapter.

The first of Melville's two chapters on Indian-hating (xxvi–xxvii, 203–20) deals with what the judge calls the "metaphysics" of Indian-hating. The use of this word is no accident. Since metaphysics deals with what transcends concrete experience and perceived reality, Melville's hint to the reader is that the judge's ideas cannot meet the test of empirical verfication. Judge Hall's discussion of the Indian-hater *par excellence* and of Indian-hating "in its perfection" will voice abstract conceptions of his own creation; his subsequent story of Moredock will be an attempt to make it appear that his metaphysical notions have a material base.

Noble reports that the judge always began his discussion by stating that the backwoodsman's hatred of the Indian has been a topic of some remark since "Indian rapine" has mostly ceased. The "philanthropist" wonders why the backwoodsman still regards the redman "in much the same spirit that a jury does a murderer, or a trapper a wild cat—a creature, in whose behalf mercy were not wisdom; truce is vain; he must be executed" (203).

To clarify this matter the judge will shortly explain his ideas about what manner of man the backwoodsman is: "as for what manner of man the Indian is, many know, either from history or experience." In this way he conveys that the Indian is so notorious it is unnecessary to elaborate upon the common idea of what he is—an idea, Hall says, largely gotten from "history." He does, however, develop at great length his ideas about what manner of man the Indian-killer is. The "backwoodsman," as he prefers to call him, is "impulsive." He is "what some might call" unprincipled. The judge compares him with those whom history looks upon as heroes: "Though held in a sort a barbarian, the backwoodsman would seem to America what Alexander was to Asia—captain in the vanguard of conquering civilization." He compares him with Hannibal, Julius Caesar, Moses in the Exodus. But he compares Indians only with those history agrees are villains.

The judge admits that a moralizer would find it terrible that a man should hate a whole race. But he excuses the Indian-hater, since he is what his education has trained him to be. It is thought best to teach the child of a backwoodsman what he must expect from an Indian. The emphasis is mine, to highlight Melville's way of speaking through the judge:

> For however charitable it may be to view Indians as members of the Society of Friends, yet to affirm them such *to one ignorant of Indians, whose lonely path lies a long way through their lands, this, in the event, might prove not only injudicious but cruel.* At least something of this kind would seem the maxim upon which backwoods' education is based. Accordingly, if in youth the backwoodsman incline to knowledge, as is generally the case, he hears little from his schoolmasters, the old chroniclers of the forest, but histories of Indian lying, Indian theft, Indian double-dealing, Indian fraud and perfidy, Indian want of conscience, Indian blood-thirstiness, Indian diabolism—*histories which, though of wild woods, are almost as full of things unangelic as the Newgate Calendar or the Annals of Europe.* In these Indian narratives and traditions the lad is thoroughly grounded. "As the twig is bent the tree's inclined." The instinct of antipathy against an Indian grows in the backwoodsman with the sense of good and bad, right and wrong. In one breath he learns that a brother is to be loved, and an Indian to be hated. (206)

The contradiction between the idea of "instinct" and of bending the twig should be noted. So should this one. Judge Hall presents the separation of human beings into brothers and Indians as a simple fact; he does not say or imply that he thinks the backwoodsman should be taught brotherhood. But later, when the band of Indians who killed Moredock's mother and her other children is under consideration, the judge speaks of them as "a gang of Cains"—a one-way conception of fraternal responsibility that lights the judge's bias: Indian-killing by the backwoodsman is the killing of a wild animal; the killing of whites by Indians is fratricide. (See p. 104-5 for a similar double standard implied in *Benito Cereno.*)

What Melville thinks about such generalizations as those about "Indian lying, Indian theft, Indian double-dealing, Indian fraud and perfidy, Indian want of conscience, Indian blood-thirstiness,

Indian diabolism" is implied in the judge's unconscious answers to
these racial accusations—answers Melville smuggles into the
judge's narration. Some of the implied answers are stated by the
judge as commonplaces without deep meaning, to be passed over
matter-of-factly, as, for example, that the backwoodsman's path
lies a long way "through their lands," that is, Indian lands. It is
Melville's reminder to the reader that the white man is an in-
truder. But the most interesting of the answers buried in the
judge's words are those implied by the comparisons he uses to show
in what an evil light the Indian is painted. He can convey the idea
of "Indian" evil only by comparison, and the comparisons are all
with non-Indians! After he states that histories of Indian evil are
"almost as full of things unangelic as the Newgate Calendar or the
Annals of Europe," he proceeds to further comparisons—again
with whites. The Indian is "now an assassin like a New York
rowdy; now a treaty-breaker like an Austrian; now a Palmer with
poisoned arrows; now a judicial murderer and Jeffries, after a
fierce farce of trial condemning his victim to bloody death." Mocmohoc, the worst historical example of "Indian treachery" the
judge can find, was deemed "a savage almost perfidious as Caesar
Borgia."

Although the judge does not realize it, the comparisons clearly
deride the idea of an "Indian" evil where Melville is concerned.
Yet one commentator speaks of the "red devils" in this story, and
another thinks of all Indians in the entire book as representing
Evil's "real home." The phrase "red devils" never appears in the
story: it is not used even by the judge or Noble. Even in the judge's
account, actual violent deeds by Indians are limited to two, the
killing of Moredock's family by a band of Indians outlawed by
their tribes, and Mocmohoc's killing of a family of cousins who had
settled on the land of his tribe. On the other hand, Moredock kills
unceasingly, his passion being to exterminate a race. Still, no critic
speaks of Moredock's race as "white devils." The idea of "red devils," read into the Indian-killer story, is an indication of how thoroughly much of American "history" has disseminated the idea of
the Indian as a devil, the very idea Melville mocks in the comparisons he puts into the mouth of Judge Hall and explodes in the
whole caricatural section on Indian-killing.

The judge goes on to say that the charitable may think that the backwoodsman does the Indian "some injustice" in thinking of him "in every evil light." The judge washes his hands of the responsibility for making any judgment (the emphasis is mine):

> Certain it is, the Indians themselves think so; quite unanimously, too. The Indians, indeed, protest against the backwoodsman's view of them; and some think that one cause of their returning his antipathy so sincerely as they do, is their moral indignation at being so libeled by him, as they really believe and say. *But whether, on this or any point, the Indians should be permitted to testify for themselves, to the exclusion of other testimony, is a question that may be left to the Supreme Court.* (208)

The judge is frankly not interested in including the testimony of the Indians; his desire is to present the white man's testimony alone. But Melville wants to remind the reader that in reality the Indian has not been allowed to testify for himself at all and that the view presented by the "historian" has been exclusively the white man's view. In having the judge raise the question of whether the Indian should be permitted to testify "to the exclusion of other testimony," Melville is employing irony to convey the fact that the real situation is the opposite: that it is the white man who has been permitted to testify "to the exclusion of other testimony" and that the view that prevails in the usual histories of the frontier is that of the society that has been the victor in the unequal war against the Indian. In the judge's story the Indian-hater wants to exterminate the Indian; in Melville's undercover account, the Indian-hater's "historian" wants to erase the Indian's true history.

The judge then tells the story of the Wrights and the Weavers who were lured to a remote part of Kentucky by the "ever-beckoning seductions of a fertile and virgin land," there to be killed by stratagem by Mocmohoc, chief of a "dwindled" tribe. Melville does not elaborate on the idea of a "dwindled" tribe, crediting the reader with the ability to understand how the tribe was dwindled by earlier invaders of their territory. The judge does not consider any such circumstance. Instead he begins his recital with an imaginary dialogue between a backwoodsman and a questioner. In what he imagines the backwoodsman to say he reveals his own thought that no matter how kind some Indians may be, it is necessary to distrust all, since there is an "Indian nature," and in the least harmful may lie the germ of a Mocmohoc. He advances the opinion that a friendly Indian is friendly only from fear. Yet immediately thereafter, without thinking of the meaning beneath his words, he voices his knowledge that the Indian who is hostile has been "turned" into an enemy and will therefore fight back now or later. The backwoodsman, he says, thinks of the friendly Indian in this way: *"Take my rifle from me, give him motive, and what will come? Or if not so, how know I what involuntary preparations may be going on in him for things as unbeknown in present time to him as me—a sort of chemical preparation in the soul for malice, as chemical preparation in the body for malady"* (my emphasis). Noble unwittingly recognizes that the judge is imposing his own thoughts on the backwoodsman: "Not that the backwoodsman ever used those words, you see, but the judge found him expression for his meaning." In an inverse way Melville finds expression for his own meaning in the words he gives to the judge.

The next subject of the judge's discussion is "the Indian-hater *par excellence,*" the judge's own metaphysical ideal. He is the one who, "having with his mother's milk drank in small love for red men, in youth or early manhood, ere the sensibilities become osseous, receives at their hand some signal outrage, or, which in effect is the same, some of his kin have, or some friend." Through this comment Melville casts doubt on the belief that the feelings of the Indian-hater do actually have their origin in personal experience, for the phrase "drank in with his mother's milk" implies the origin of Indian-hating to precede experience. Then Melville dilutes even the idea of an outstanding individual trauma as the basis for the passion of Indian-hating by the diminuendo from "some signal outrage" to "some of his kin" to "some friend." Then, by having the judge tell his audience matter-of-factly that Indian-hating develops such attractions for the Indian-hater *par excellence* that thoughts of other outrages he has suffered—not connected with Indians—"troop to the nucleus thought, assimilate with it, and swell it," Melville is all but telling the reader that the Indian has become the socially acceptable scapegoat for other difficulties the white man encounters, of completely different origin. But the judge again ignores the significance of what he has said. Suddenly he metamorphoses the idea of a particular outrage into the idea of a guilty race: the Indian-hater *par excellence* makes a vow, "the hate of which is a vortex from whose suction scarce the remotest chip of the guilty race may reasonably feel secure." The Indian-hater *par excellence* then takes leave of his kin, commits himself to the forest primeval, and dedicates his life to implacable and lonesome vengeance. The judge believes that in "the highest view" such a soul is one that peeps out but once in an age. Other Indian-haters are not able to withstand so well the need human beings have of each other. Noble tells the confidence-man about examples the judge would bring forward to illustrate the average Indian-hater's need for human contact. To Judge Hall the need is an "infirmity." But the paragraph is an oblique expression of the idea that the human race is one, and men do need each other.

> The judge, with his usual judgment, always thought that the intense solitude to which the Indian-hater consigns himself, has, by its overawing influence, no little to do with relaxing his vow. He would relate instances where, after some months' lonely scoutings, the Indian-hater is suddenly seized with a sort of calenture; hurries openly towards the first smoke, though he knows it is an Indian's, announces himself as a lost hunter, gives the savage his rifle, throws himself upon his charity, embraces him with much affection, imploring the privilege of living a while in his sweet companionship. (213)

The Indian-killer who must return from time to time to domestic life is what the judge calls a diluted Indian-hater. He deplores the fact that this man finds the call of others irresistible. But it appears that the diluted Indian-hater has his uses; he is the one who, "by his very infirmity, enables us to form surmises, however inadequate, of what Indian-hating in its perfection is." The distinction is now clear: the Indian-hater *par excellence* is a standard of "perfection"; a biography of him is unimaginable, as the judge admits. A diluted Indian-hater like Moredock is a more credible figure having some connection with actuality. Such a man can become a folk hero, one who is imaginable, one in whom the judge's audience can believe and with whom they can identify.

The title of the chapter in which the judge, after the long orientation of his audience, finally arrives at the biography of Moredock (215–20) characterizes its subject as "a man of questionable morality." The title and hence the characterization are Melville's. The judge does *not* raise the question of Moredock's morality; indeed, no aspect of Moredock is too bizarre for him to accept matter-of-factly, or to excuse. Behavior and feeling departing most markedly from the normal are reported admiringly by him. The chapter is a marvel of grotesquerie by means of which Melville shows the monstrous nature of the judge's kind of history.

The judge begins Moredock's history with a tribute to the memory of this man. He asks the company to join him in a few moments of "deep silence and deeper reverie" while they puff on their cigars: "Gentlemen, let us smoke to the memory of Colonel John Moredock." He explains, "Though Colonel John Moredock was not an Indian-hater *par excellence,* he yet cherished a kind of sentiment towards the red man, and in that degree, and so acted out his sentiment as sufficiently to merit the tribute just rendered to his memory."

According to the judge's story, Moredock was the son of a mother "thrice widowed by a tomahawk" who continued west to the frontier where she and all her nine children but John were slaughtered when a band of twenty Indians, "renegades from various tribes," attacked and killed the party of westward-moving settlers of which she and her children were a part. John was saved only by the fact that he had been with a second party following some fifty miles behind. "Other youngsters might have turned mourners; he turned avenger." He set out to discover who the actual culprits were. They proved to belong to a marauding band, outlaws among Indians, whom Moredock trailed for more than a year. Then he and his men succeeded in killing all but three of them. These three Moredock pursued for three more years until he had killed them all.

> All were now dead. But this did not suffice. He made no avowal, but to kill Indians had become his passion. . . . The

solitary Indian that met him died. . . . Many years he spent
thus; and though after a time he was, in a degree, restored to
the ordinary life of the region and period, yet it is believed
that John Moredock never let pass an opportunity of quench-
ing an Indian. Sins of commission in that kind may have been
his, but none of omission. (217–18)

Yet, says the judge, Moredock was not naturally ferocious or
possessed of those qualities that tend to withdraw a man from
social life. "On the contrary, Moredock was an example of something apparently self-contradicting, certainly curious, but, at the
same time, undeniable: namely, that nearly all Indian-haters have
at bottom loving hearts." He goes on to a description of Moredock
that recalls Melville's satirical account of the grandfather in *Pierre*
who annihilated two Indians by bludgeoning their heads together,
"and all this was done by the mildest hearted, and most blue-eyed
gentleman in the world, . . . the gentlest husband and the gentlest
father; the kindest of masters to his slaves." Moredock, similarly,

> showed himself not without humane feelings. No cold hus-
> band or colder father, he; and though often and long away
> from his household, bore its needs in mind, and provided for
> them. He could be very convivial; told a good story (though
> never of his more private exploits), and sung a capital song.
> Hospitable, not backward to help a neighbor; by report, be-
> nevolent, as retributive, in secret . . . yet with nobody, Indians
> excepted, otherwise than courteous in a manly fashion; a moc-
> casined gentleman, admired and loved. (218)

At one time, being urged to become a candidate for governor of
Illinois, Moredock declined without giving reasons, but the judge
explains for him. The emphasis is mine to call attention to Melville's way of mocking the judge through his choice of words:

> In his official capacity he might be called upon to enter into
> friendly treaties with Indian tribes, a thing not to be thought
> of. And even did no such contingency arise, yet he felt there

would be *impropriety* in the Governor of Illinois stealing out now and then, during a recess of the legislative bodies, for *a few days' shooting* at human beings, within the limits of his paternal chief-magistracy. If the governorship offered large honors, from Moredock it demanded larger *sacrifices. . . .* In short, he was not unaware that to be a consistent Indian-hater involves the renunciation of ambition, with its objects—the pomps and glories of the world; and since religion, pronouncing such things vanities, accounts it merit to renounce them, therefore, so far as this goes, Indian-hating, whatever may be thought of it in other respects, may be regarded as not wholly without the efficacy of a devout sentiment. (219-20)

This concludes the account by a man misnamed "Noble" of a memorized "history" originally told as if to the press and to others with "impressible" memories. Obviously, it does not in any particular correspond to Melville's idea, at this time or at any other, of what the real history of the white man and the Indian in America was. The judge's verdict on this aspect of American history, his tribute to the Indian-hater/Indian-killer, completely contradicts what Melville says—in an explicit way—in every other work in which this issue or any closely related one arises. *Typee* (1846) refers with indignation to the Anglo-Saxons who have "extirpated the greater portion of the Red race" from the North American continent. It speaks with admiration of the courage of the American Indian, condemns invaders who make native people into "interlopers" in the land of their fathers, and names the vindictiveness with which white men carry on their wars—the exact theme of the Moredock story in *The Confidence-Man*—as that which distinguishes "the white civilized man as the most ferocious animal on the face of the earth." *Mardi* (1849) says of Vivenza (the United States): "Not yet wholly extinct were its aboriginal people . . . who year by year were driven further and further into remoteness till, as one of their sad warriors said, after continual removes along the log, his race was almost on the point of being pushed off the end," and there is a reference to "poor Logan, last of his tribe" (the Iroquois Indian, who advocated peaceful and friendly relations with the white settlers), all of whose family was killed by whites. *Moby-Dick* (1850) refers to the Puritans' superstition that the Indian is a son of Satan; yet one of the interpreters of the Moredock story offers this reference in *Moby-Dick* as evidence to support the contention that all references to Indians in *The Confidence-Man* should be understood as references to Evil. The "Supplement" to *Battle-Pieces* (1866) talks of the exterminating hate of race toward race, another way of stating the theme of the Moredock chapter. In *Clarel* (1876) the part-Indian Ungar says the Anglo-Saxons are hated by myriads of Indians "East and West," who have been "dispossessed of rights"; he calls the Anglo-Saxons "pirates of the sphere" and "grave, canting Mammonite free-booters," who, in the name of Christianity and Trade, would "deflower the world's last sylvan glade"; he describes the Indian's "hopeless" state under the white's "aggressive reign." *John Marr* (1888) again asserts Melville's consistent, lifelong position; it tells of the prairie with its "remnant of Indians thereabout—all but exterminated in their recent but final war with regular white troops, a war waged by the Red Men for their native soil and natural rights."

But, says the argument in the dominant critical literature on the Indian-hating section, Melville could champion the Indian cause in real life and yet choose the Indian as his symbol of evil in an imaginative work. But the poetic imagination does not work in such a way. No precedents can be cited of a poet choosing a people he considers wronged in history as his symbol of Evil in a work devoted to that history. Can one conceive of this parallel situation—that a creative writer appalled at the fate of the Jews under the Nazis should choose the Jew as his symbol of Evil in a work dealing with that very genocide? The theory that Melville did the equivalent of this has no real basis. It grows out of the related theory, also without foundation, that Melville had a conception of an absolutely abstract Evil divorced from its manifestations in the life of human beings. Not only was Melville's attitude toward the white man's war on the Indian consistent throughout his life, but the Indian-hating section of *The Confidence-Man* is the high point of his writing on this subject. Beneath its grotesque mask one sees, if one looks, Melville's expression of horror at the vindictiveness with which the white man has carried on his war against the Indian, that vindictiveness that makes the white civilized man "the most ferocious animal on the face of the earth." Beneath the judge's "history" that pays tribute to a life devoted to genocide lies Melville's idea that the judge's tale, with its "metaphysical" introduction, recounted by the hypocritical Noble, is representative of "History's" attempt to ennoble this ignoble chapter in America's story.

This interpretation of the chapters on Indian-hating is substantiated first by the links between this section and others in the jigsaw puzzle and second by the unique and key role played by this section in *The Confidence-Man* picture as a whole. An examination of these two kinds of relationship—with other parts and with the whole—confirms that the Moredock story represents the false face of innocence that "history" has placed over the deeds committed by American civilization through its deputy, the Indian-killer.

Though the idea of sinning by deputy is the main link uniting the section on Indian-hating, the section about the man with clean hands, and the section dealing with the mystic philosopher and his practical disciple, there are other points of connection. The man with clean hands contributes money to a fund to help the widows and orphans of the Seminole Indians (killed in what some history books call the Seminole War, which is described in the *Encyclopedia Americana* as "the fiercest of all wars waged by the United States upon the Indians"). The Moredock story casts an ironic light back on this charitable contribution by the man with immaculate hands. A similar link joins, at another point, the Moredock piece of the puzzle and the mystic philosopher piece. The mystic philosopher indirectly expresses, through a question to the confidence-man, his own intense desire to be like the snake, to be able to kill and yet not be held responsible. He would like to be an "iridescent scabbard of death," that is, able to send forth a deadly sword, yet remain himself shining and jewel-like. And so it is, in the Indian-killing section, with conquering American civilization: it has the deed done but acts a part charitable and "noble." A further bond between the Moredock and Winsome pieces lies in the idea that just as Winsome provides his practical disciple with high-sounding theoretical justification for shabby deeds, so the judge-historian provides "historical" justification for Indian-killing, naming it vengeance and ignoring the real origins of the conflict. And just as the mystic Winsome leaves the scene as soon as his disciple enters, not wanting to hear what is done in his name, so American society, with the help of the judge's "history," hides from the knowledge that what is being done is being done for it. If it can remain ignorant, it may be found innocent and thus escape the consequences of the acts it approves.

An engaging question, tacitly raised by Melville and left unanswered for the reader to puzzle out, also connects the section about the mystic and his disciple with the Moredock section. The confidence-man persists in calling the mystic's disciple "Charlie," although his name is Egbert. Why does he call him by Noble's name? To what meaning and to what link between the sections does this point? The answer to the question must lie in similarities between the two "Charlies" and what each says. Egbert is the character who tells the other lengthy story in *The Confidence-Man*. It is the story of China Aster and it is told to justify Egbert's refusal— in the name of friendship and in the spirit of his master's essay on friendship—to lend or give money to a friend. It resembles the Moredock story in that it also is a memorized account originally told by someone else, and it, too, expresses Melville's ideas indirectly. The echo of Polonius in Egbert's thinking again links him with Noble, who had earlier spoken hypocritically in criticism of Polonius but who acts just like Egbert about lending or giving money. Egbert's story of China Aster is Melville's way of reflecting upon the character of Egbert, upon the philosophy he serves, or that serves him, and upon other narrators who spread similar self-justificatory ideas. This story is also a mask, intended to conceal Egbert's real motivation, which is pure and simple stinginess. Correspondingly, the story of Moredock reveals the character of Noble, of the judge, of the society they both represent, and of the kind of history they transmit. It, too, is a false face, intended to cover the real motivation for Indian-killing in American history—pure and simple determination to seize the Indians' lands. By having the confidence-man misname Egbert "Charlie," Melville flashes a signal calling the reader's attention to the interconnections between the two long narratives, to the spurious philosophies they both serve, and to the similar underlying motivations they try to conceal.

The ways in which other portions of the puzzle interlock with the Moredock portion highlight various facets of the judge's mode of narrating history and link him with other "white operators" in the masquerade on the *Fidèle*. Passages elsewhere on one-sidedness dovetail with the one-sidedness of his type of history, paralyzed all down one side. The crippled "soldier's" habit of telling the kind of story that will get him the response he wants parallels the judge's way of relating history. The barber's supplying of false mustaches, wigs, dyes, and cosmetics to give people a disguised appearance mirrors the judge's dressing up or hiding the real face of Indian-killing. Taking the judge's kind of history at face value is one of the kinds of foolish trust against which *The Confidence-Man* warns.

In the light that is thrown back and forth between the Moredock section and *The Confidence-Man* as a whole, we find insights into both the part and the whole. The Moredock account deals with both past and present—the war of white America against the American Indian for the Indian's land was still going on at the time of the book—and, for Melville, the true story beneath its distortion has significance for the country's future as well. The composite picture of *The Confidence-Man* is a portrayal of a society that hides its nature. Masquerading as a civilization, it actually lives by the law of the jungle. The Indian-killer is openly what the civilization is in disguise: "in new countries, where the wolves are killed off, the foxes increase," the book hints at the start, and the main fox is the society itself. It is also its own victim, keeping itself from self-knowledge.

As the whole of *The Confidence-Man* irradiates the Indian-hating section, the light radiating from the Indian-hating section increases the total illumination, in this sense: it is the only "history," the only backward look at America, in the work. Stripped of the mask behind which the judge falsifies the significance of Indian-killing, it is Melville's view of the connection between the past, the present, and the future. Indian-killing is implied to be not only a manifestation of the lack of morality in the *Fidèle* society; it is one of the main reasons why the society has become what it is. The masking, from the beginning of its history, of moral questions such as those involved in its relations with the Indian (as with the black man), the placing of the desire for gain above all else (for territory in the one case, as for profit in the other), are hinted to have been factors that fostered, from the start, the growth of hypocrisy and corruption; the early disregard of morality in regard to the Indian set a pattern that then became predominant in relations between white and white. As for the future, the words that Noble quotes from the judge, even before the two chapters on the Indian-hater begin, show that the story is told not only to justify the policy of the past and present but to make it certain that it will be the policy of the future. The judge's early words, "And Indian-hating still exists; and, no doubt, will continue to exist, so long as Indians do," take on a new, more sinister meaning when the whole book has been read, for it is clear then that the judge is not making a sad prediction but setting forth the doctrine of race extermination. He can be seen, then, to have expressed from the beginning the view of a destroyer master race. This sentence sets the tone for his narration of the events of history told from the victorious white man's angle, while things to which the Indian himself might testify "may be left to the Supreme Court." On rereading, this remark—in the total context that shows the United States traveling blindly from flawed past to ugly present to catastrophic future—makes one wonder which Supreme Court Melville, not the judge, has in mind. Is it the United States Supreme Court of the 1850s or is it the "heavenly tribunal" of which White-Jacket speaks in the chapter about his arraignment at the mast?

So in yet another Melville work the idea in the footnote in *Omoo* is echoed, that war being the greatest of evils, all its "accessories" necessarily partake of the same evil. In the Indian-hating section of *The Confidence-Man* the war is the war of white America against the American Indian, and the "historian" is its accessory.

Notes

1. Herman Melville, *The Confidence-Man: His Masquerade,* ed. H. Bruce Franklin (Indianapolis: Bobbs-Merrill, 1967). All page references that follow in the text are to this edition.

2. For an excellent summary of the facts known about the state of Melville's mind, health, and finances in this two-year period, see Elizabeth S. Foster's "Introduction" in *The Confidence-Man* (New York: Hendricks, 1954), pp. xx–xxiv.

3. The outstanding exception is Roy Harvey Pearce's view in "Melville's Indian-hater: A Note on a Meaning of *The Confidence-Man, PMLA,* 67 (1952), 942–48, and in the chapter "The Metaphysics of Indian-hating: Leatherstocking Unmasked" in his book, *The Savages of America: The American Indian and the Idea of Civilization* (Baltimore: The Johns Hopkins Univ. Press, 1953).

4. See Foster's "Introduction," p. xlviii, for Melville's expression of opinion in his review in 1849 of Parkman's *Oregon Trail.*

5. Excerpts from James Hall's writings appear in Foster's "Explanatory Notes" at the end of the Hendricks House edition of *The Confidence-Man,* pp. 334–38. It is necessary to go to the original for the chapter called "Indian-hating" in *The Wilderness and the War Path* (New York, 1846). The latter makes it most clear that the real Hall, though he regrets the situation in the West, was nevertheless an apologist for the white American's war on the American Indian.

8.

Battle-Pieces: Melville's Historic Tragedy
of the Civil War

Not until the end of the prose supplement to *Battle-Pieces* [1] did Melville's idea of the Civil War as tragedy, in the literary sense, surface in words, in the prayer that "the terrible [2] historic tragedy of our time may not have been enacted without instructing our whole beloved country through terror and pity." But that conception permeates the work from "The Portent" through "America," making it, in essence, a tragic drama. Melville comes close to saying this was his intention when, also in the "Supplement," he describes the action of *Battle-Pieces* as having presented "dramatically" the passions of the war. The tragic conception unifies poems written in "moods variable, and at times widely at variance" and is the basis for the "order" into which the pieces "naturally fall" [3]— the three-part causal sequence that is characteristic of tragedy: origin and building up of the fate; agony; enlightenment. The work encompasses thoughts about many philosophical questions— among them uncertainties about the nature of man, the connections between Death and Life, and the relation between the tragic events "of our time" and the universe—but the heart of *Battle-Pieces* is Melville's feeling about America's historic tragedy; all rays out from—and does not exist apart from—that intense concern.

133

To see *Battle-Pieces* as tragic in its conception is to have a view of its philosophy and art different from that of theologically minded interpreters to whom Melville's thought is essentially abstract and ahistorical and to whom the work is, above all, a statement of a credo: that the universe is evil and the Civil War only another manifestation of its malevolence. For tragedy focuses on man: on his or her potentialities for destructive or creative action; his passions; his possibilities of disintegration or growth; the extent of, and the limitations upon, his ability to govern his life; the conflicts within him; and the organic connections between past, present, and future. These are the questions with which *Battle-Pieces* wrestles: its vitality arises from the fact that man, acting in time and place, able only to speculate about the cosmos, is the center of Melville's artistic universe. Had the answer to all his questions been that "evil is the permanent and controlling reality," [4]—a theory that robs tragedy of meaning—he would have found the cause of all wars to be one. But he, who hated the very idea of war, felt that the Civil War had a special historical necessity. This sense of its difference from other wars he had condemned unconditionally was the cause of the inner war that informs *Battle-Pieces*.

The power of tragedy depends to a great extent on a choice demanded in a paradoxical situation. Such a choice and situation confronted Melville at the time of the Civil War. No longer could he warn simultaneously against slavery and war. The storm he had predicted in *Mardi* had become an actuality; the sleeping volcano in *Benito Cereno* (which reappears in *Battle-Pieces*) had erupted. So Melville was presented with a contradiction rich in tragic possibilities, stated simply in the "Supplement": that since emancipation was not accomplished by deliberate legislation, "only through agonized violence could so mighty a result be effected," that is, only through the "greatest of evils" (as war is described in *Omoo*) could "man's foulest crime" (as slavery is named in "Misgivings") be abolished. This contradiction between the Civil War and War gives *Battle-Pieces* its tension, "suspense," and emotional power.

On the one hand, Melville makes clear in the strongest possible terms his moral stand on the basic issue of the war. In poem after poem God is the image standing for the "Right" that the Union upholds, Satan the image signifying the "Wrong" for which the South is fighting. The North is the "just one" in a war forced upon it. However brave the young southern soldiers may prove, however tainted northern virtue may show itself to be, as in the New York draft riots, the spirit that urges the North is "divine" while the "evil end" of the South is the continued rule of Lucifer. Allusions to the Bible and *Paradise Lost* serve to dramatize the moral issues; if Melville thinks it necessary, he transforms the original conception, as in the case of his Satan, who retains none of the aura of rebellious beauty and heroism of Milton's.

And yet, Melville cannot put out of his mind War's "theft" of life and youth, the death list that "like a river flows," and "blood, and tears, and anguished War!" The pain in the poetry is not for Northern youth alone but for all the young soldiers "swept by the wind of their place and time." [5] The "whole beloved country" can be understood to be the tragic figure from the first mention of the "country's ills" to the drama's end, in which America assumes a single human form.

The tragedy falls into three "acts." The first reminds us that slavery is the origin of the tragic fate and brings that fate steadily closer. The second enacts the agony of the war. The third culminates in the illumination and look to the future with which tragedy traditionally ends.

Battle-Pieces opens with what is essentially a dramatic prologue, an introductory scene that is also a historical prelude to the events to follow. In the first edition a special role of "The Portent" is clearly implied: it is separated from the rest of the poems by a blank page; it is not listed in the "Contents"; it alone of the poems is in italic type throughout. The title, the date beneath it, and the poem line by line, affirm the dramatic purpose of the scene on which the curtain rises. The place is the green Shenandoah Valley, soon to be wasted by war. The time is just after the execution of John Brown, the most dramatic antislavery figure of the time.

The Portent.
(1859.)

Hanging from the beam,
  Slowly swaying (such the law),

Gaunt the shadow on your green,
*   Shenandoah!*
The cut is on the crown
(Lo, John Brown),
And the stabs shall heal no more.

Hidden in the cap
*   Is the anguish none can draw;*
So your future veils its face,
*   Shenandoah!*
But the streaming beard is shown
(Weird John Brown),
The meteor of the war.

In this spare fourteen-line poem Melville captures "the future in the instant," [6] a remarkable aim, remarkably achieved. Although nothing actually happens or seems to change in the moment on which Melville's imagination concentrates, the scene is in motion. It compels us to see the passage of time even as we see the arrest of time for the suspended body of John Brown. Melville creates the impression of the future moving within the present by opposing the effects of sight and sound. The retarded tempo imposed by the prolonged sounds of the words in every line except the last holds back, seems even to stop, time. The drawn-out refrain, "Shenandoah!" echoed by the mournful "No more" and "war," has the effect of a bell tolling death. But the visual image evoked by the slowly moving lines gives the effect of time relentlessly advancing, no matter how Brown's executioners may have thought to stop it dead. Intrinsic to the back-and-forth pendulum image communicated by the dragging but regular beat of "slowly swaying" is the idea of the inexorable passing of time and, in the full context of the poem, of the fatal wasting of time while, with each sway of the pendulum, the waste of war comes nearer. We are compelled to see, at one and the same moment, the present green and the future brown [7] of the Shenandoah Valley. We are led to sense many a death to come at the same time as we look up at the one dead body before us. As the pendulum sways (to sway means also to exert an influence), fate is approaching; time is passing in which a law to end slavery could be, but will not be enacted; instead, "such the law" that Brown, who as a meteor is associated with heaven, has been executed. Passage of time is implicit, too, in the attenuating shadow on the green. By calling Brown "weird," Melville makes his hanged body a prophecy, the man a prophet, and the future foreseen the country's fate: the word, derived from Old English *wyrd,* may mean either fate, prophecy, or seer. Combining all three senses of *weird,* Melville makes his transition to the last line in which Brown's body (his beard is a synecdoche) is openly said to be the portent of the war. (At this moment one can be virtually sure that the poem originated in Melville's imagination with the conception of the high hanged figure as a heavenly body that, for a moment, when it enters the atmosphere, leaves behind a streak of light.) In the closing line, sound and image at last coincide. The tempo of the word "meteor," the movement of the image it evokes, and the coming of the fate—all are now swift, and we are propelled into the future. There follows only the closing chord, the word "war" finally spoken. The poem's ending announces the drama's beginning.

The first act opens with "Misgivings." The scene, a composite one of hills, valley, town, lone mountain in the background, with the seashore suggested farther off, is symbolic of the country. Two years after the event pictured in "The Portent," even a child may see war coming.

Misgivings.
(1860.)

When ocean-clouds over inland hills
   Sweep storming in late autumn brown,
And horror the sodden valley fills,
   And the spire falls crashing in the town,
I muse upon my country's ills—
The tempest bursting from the waste of Time
On the world's fairest hope linked with man's foulest
     crime.

Nature's dark side is heeded now—
  (Ah! optimist-cheer disheartened flown)—
A child may read the moody brow
  Of yon black mountain lone.
With shouts the torrents down the gorges go,
And storms are formed behind the storm we feel:
The hemlock shakes in the rafter, the oak in the
      driving keel.

Again Melville's acute sense of time passing shapes the poetry. Again the future is contained in the present, although until the storms form behind the one all feel, the scene seems only ordinarily symbolic of approaching war; but with the climax in the last three lines we discover that the poem duplicates what it envisions—the process of building up toward collapse. The rafter supporting the roof already contains the weakness that will cause the house to fall; that the house signifies the country that "cannot stand" would be clear to contemporaries of Lincoln. The ship, for which the keel is a synecdoche, drives on, as time is driving on, to break up; the ship would be understood to be the "ship of state," which Longfellow had not long before said, in reference to America, held the hopes of humanity hanging breathless on her fate and which Sophocles in *Antigone* said the gods had put back on an even keel after the "stormy surge." (Melville owned works by both poets.) [8]

But in "Misgivings" the stirring of the past in the present is equally important. The poet who muses about his "country's ills" is, we know, a player with words; he is speaking of the current trouble of the country and at the same time of past ills responsible for those of the present. The "waste of Time," too, has no single meaning. Since it echoes so closely Shakespeare's "dear time's waste" in Sonnet xxx, which also summons up remembrance of the past (Merton Sealts's *Melville's Reading* lists a separate volume of the *Sonnets* among the books Melville owned), the phrase in "Misgivings" implies first the squandering of precious time in the past and the wasting away of remaining time. A second implication is that America may become part of the waste (the debris) of Time, not because man's hopes are inevitably doomed, but because the "world's fairest hope" was linked from the start with "man's foulest crime." The spire "falls crashing," conveying, in the total context, that the church also, since it countenanced or could not end the crime of slavery, suffered from the same flaw as the country. Moreover the waste already accumulated is explosive, like the volcano in "The Apparition"; the tempest is "bursting" from the continued ill. *Waste* suggests, too, that the country is a stretch of uncultivated land; slavery, *Mardi* says, puts out the sun at noon and parches all fertility, and Melville regularly thinks in related images of clouds and shadow and brown, as he does here, when slavery is either his subject or an intrinsic part of it. What is not implied, either within the context of the whole poem or the whole of *Battle-Pieces*, is that time in itself "is a process of attrition and decay" that suddenly " 'bursts' forth to destroy the best that man has been able to create." [9]

"Misgivings" reveals also the past in the *future*, where it may be the main factor causing collapse. The hemlock in the rafter, like the oak in the keel, is timber from the past. Strong as they are, they shake. Something even stronger was needed to insure the future of the country than what went into its construction. Melville's misgivings are not so much about whether the storm of war is coming—of that there can be no doubt—but about the ability of the nation so constructed to survive it.

"Misgivings," then, names the tragic flaw that is the cause of the dramatic events to come. By naming the flaw it makes the meaning of "Right" and "Wrong," words so much a part of the vocabulary of the drama, unmistakable. Even in the scenes in which there is no allusion to slavery, "man's foulest crime" remains in our minds as the essential background of the tragedy because of its importance in the imagery and development of "Misgivings."

Its form, an almost musical arrangement of voices, conveys the aim of "The Conflict of Convictions," subtitled "1860-1." Thoughts inevitably activated at that time are counterpointed in the first thirteen stanzas, which alternate ordinary and italic type. The "stage" is unlighted; only voices are heard. During most of this piece of the historic tragedy two voices, one of which may be an inner voice, express increasing pessimism. They brood over whether war must come to America; whether there is a God with power and ultimately creative purpose; whether man's heart is changeless and hence "Time's strand" necessarily strewn with wrecks; whether the hopes of the past perished because it "drudged through pain and crime" or because Death inevitably negates all human efforts. The colloquy moves from some attempt on the part of each speaker to find a reason to have faith in the future, to sheer pessimism, to a silence like that of death. Then a third voice enters to hover for a moment over the invisible scene. It speaks in all capital letters. We might think it the voice of ultimate Truth, except that Melville did not believe in any, and a banal conception of final Truth it would be; moreover he did believe, as one knows from "Misgivings," that by 1860–1 prophecy was all too possible. Whose voice, then, is the final one?

> YEA AND NAY—
> EACH HATH HIS SAY;
> BUT GOD HE KEEPS THE MIDDLE WAY.
> NONE WAS BY
> WHEN HE SPREAD THE SKY;
> WISDOM IS VAIN, AND PROPHESY.

It is the voice of the poem itself: the stanza arises from Melville's poetic and dramatic sense rather than from a need to offer a final statement about the philosophical questions. The structure reveals the poem's purpose to be the re-creation of the "gloomy lull of the early part of the winter of 1860–1" to which the short note to this poem calls attention. This lull, "seeming big with final disaster to our institutions, affected some minds that believed them to constitute one of the great hopes of mankind, much as the eclipse which came over the promise of the first French Revolution affected kindred natures, throwing them *for the time* into doubts and misgivings universal" (my emphasis). The poem imitates the lull, first by setting forth conflicting speculations that cannot be tested and resolved, and then by adding a stanza so that no note previously struck may appear to have spoken the last word. The ending, which can, according to the poem's conception, be no final statement, establishes a precarious balance. It suggests that what will follow is an ominous silence, eventually to be broken. "The

Conflict of Convictions" as an individual poem captures the feelings that existed "for the time." As part of the historic tragedy it creates the momentary pause before the event that triggers the tragic action.

"Apathy and Enthusiasm" is confirmation that the dramatic quality of the lull preceding tragic anguish was what struck Melville in relation to 1860–61. It tells of the ending of the "calm" when events suddenly "came resounding"

> With the cry that *All was lost,*
> Like the thunder-cracks of massy ice
>   In intensity of frost—
> Bursting upon one another
>   Through the horror of the calm.

The division in the nation grows "momently more wide." With Easter and spring, the icebound rivers melt. Apathy in the North gives way to elation on the part of the young after they hear "Sumter's cannon roar" and to foreboding on the part of their elders—a contrast that implies the tragic paradox that whereas enthusiasm and action are necessary in war against the "Arch-fiend," innumerable young men in the spring of their lives will not survive to summer. Melville gives them the quality that Shakespeare gave Romeo and Juliet—the often fatal impulsiveness of youth. The poem is a prophecy of grief for the older generation. The ice in the first part of the poem and Coleridge's word "momently," so rarely used, are reminders of "Kubla Khan" in which a "mighty fountain momently was forced," fragments of a chasm burst "rebounding," ancestral voices prophesied war, and "all should cry, Beware! Beware!" That the reminder was intentional is supported by the "sunny Dome" in "America." (We know from Merton Sealts's *Melville's Reading* that Melville purchased Coleridge's *Biographia Literaria* in 1848, an indication of early interest in him.)

"The March into Virginia" fully unleashes the tragic action. The rapidity of the tempo and imagery of its central section indicates the acceleration of terrible events, though the scene seems so gay:

> The banners play, the bugles call,
> The air is blue and prodigal.
>   No berrying party, pleasure-wooed,
> No picnic party in the May,
> Ever went less loth than they
>   Into that leafy neighborhood.
> In Bacchic glee they file toward Fate,
> Moloch's uninitiate;
> Expectancy, and glad surmise
> Of battle's unknown mysteries.

Ironies and ambiguities tumble over each other. To what "pleasure" are the banners and bugles wooing these boys? Are they quite ignorant or is it that they spurn wisdom? Are they, too, "prodigal," so eager are they for experience? War's mysteries are war's rites, and which so frequent as its funeral rites? That the youth go off in Bacchic glee toward Fate, as if to a berrying party (a "burying party," as Robert Penn Warren points out in his rich analysis of this poem),[10] affirms once more that the concept of tragic drama is pervasive in *Battle-Pieces*. For Melville, familiar with Aristotle's interpretation of tragedy, must have known, too, that tragedy grew out of the hymn sung at the festival to Dionysus, the Greek equivalent of Bacchus, god of fields and vineyards. "Bacchic glee," then, imparts that tragedy will replace the "rapture sharp" the soldiers feel as they eagerly march, like the boys in "Ball's Bluff," to meet death. That some of those so drunk with enthusiasm "Shall die experienced ere three days are spent— / Perish, enlightened by the vollied glare" is again a reminder of the literary form in which enlightenment and death seem simultaneous. The paradoxical question tormenting Melville in regard to the march into Virginia comes at the beginning of the poem, to which one returns at the end: If youth did not its "ignorant impulse lend," how in a situation like that in the United States at that time could the "just or larger end" be attained?

The second act progresses from defeats and victories to the eventual triumph of the North, followed immediately by the assassination of Lincoln. Virtually all of the poems in this middle section are about individual land or naval engagements and thoughts and feelings they aroused. This act best reflects the intensifying stress within Melville in the long course of the war. Against the steady drumbeats—Right / Wrong, God / Satan—strains are counterpointed that develop the theme of War and the universal suffering it brings. Realistic portrayal of war, one of the main characteristics of *Battle-Pieces* and one of its revolutionary literary aspects, has, of course, an antiwar effect. But far beyond that, the phenomenal mating of realism and symbolism for which the work should be best known bares the inner realities within actualities of battle. Ironies, contrasts. and juxtapositions of incongruous things—transformations, largely, of facts in news reports—are directed against War: names of places, the weather and other natural aspects of scenes, artifacts like a fort, a trench, a buried gun, become symbols of war. Battle images, appealing to almost every sense, especially of cold, movement, muscular tension, or visceral shock, are necessary to specific scenes and rich in larger implications.

In selecting from the more than three dozen poems in the second act of the drama, I am guided by a desire to draw attention to the counterpointing of Melville's responses to the Civil War and to War: those places where they pull against each other and those places in which they work as one. But poems not analyzed also contribute to making real to the reader what might otherwise be a very vague sense of the slaughter of the Civil War.

With bare words, a simple pictorial scene, and a final auditory image that directs the reader's thinking beyond the single occasion, Melville in "Ball's Bluff" gives a relatively small event a large significance. The first of three seven-line stanzas recalls a recent noonday sight, "saddest that eyes can see," of young soldiers marching "lustily / Unto the wars" with "fifes, and flags in mottoed pageantry." The second conveys how alive they were, how immortal they felt, how like the gods. In the last stanza the street is the same, but night has come, and silence, and Death to young soldiers in whom "Life throbbed so strong":

> Weeks passed; and at my window, leaving bed,
>   By night I mused, of easeful sleep bereft,
>   On those brave boys (Ah War! thy theft);
>   Some marching feet

Found pause at last by cliffs Potomac cleft;
    Wakeful I mused, while in the street
Far footfalls died away till none were left.

Only some of the brave boys find pause beside the Potomac; yet the far footfalls die away till none are left, so that the reader, too, will hear the fading sound carrying the sense of all youth who move "like Juny morning on the wave" dying away till all are gone if the theft of War goes on.

Inspired by the plan that led to the victory of Commander Dupont in the naval battle against the forts on both sides of Port Royal Sound, "Dupont's Round Fight" stresses the "aim" of all art, including, by implication, Dupont's, and suggesting the large aim, rather than the immediate military aim, of the elliptical route the ships took down and then up the river. This larger meaning should be clear: the ships are "the Fleet that warred for Right / And warring *so*, prevailed" (my emphasis). The geometric beauty in the orbital path symbolizes "Law," and *Law* with a capital letter has, in *Battle-Pieces*, the force of the covenant between God and Israel, the ethical Law imposed by God, who will war on the side of the righteous. Melville's intellectual conclusion comes at the beginning of the poem. It expresses his belief about poetry. For him Dupont's plan is a symbol of the unity of aim and method that art should have:

In time and measure perfect moves
    All Art whose aim is sure;
Evolving rhyme and stars divine
    Have rules, and they endure.

In accordance with the rule of unity of strategy and aim, this poem evolved a mathematical precision of meter and rhyme, a rare thing in *Battle-Pieces* but here demanded by the theme.

The twenty-page "Donelson" also evolved into a work in which content and poetic means are one. But whereas the content of "Dupont's Round Fight," being cerebral, can to an extent be paraphrased, the content of "Donelson" is emotional and cannot be paraphrased at all; it *is* the tension within Melville, pulling him back and forth between partisan support of the northern side of the "curs'd ravine" dividing the country in the Civil War and his feeling for both sides of the "curs'd ravine" that divides humanity. This tension and its artistic realization in "Donelson" have not sufficiently been noted and the poem has not received the detailed analysis given to others of the battle-pieces. Yet the time and creative effort Melville must have expended on it and the space he allotted it when he brought the pieces of the historic tragedy together—it is by far the longest poem in *Battle-Pieces*—suggest that his own imaginative, emotional, and critical commitment to it was strong. So will be that of any reader once he or she becomes aware of Melville's inner war. What will then be striking as the poem develops after the "chilly change in the afternoon" (l. 64), and especially on subsequent readings, are the poem's extraordinary blending of realism and symbolism; its original structure and development; its uses of irony, anticlimax, words with multiple connotations, and symbolic contrasts; its "cinematic" techniques; and its images that, while appealing to nearly every physical sense, appeal at the same time to our mental / emotional sense of wider implications in what is physically perceived, implications about Life, Death, Time, Nature, and the complexity of man that is brought home so sharply by the contradictions of a "just" war.

The camera shifts back and forth in "Donelson" between a street scene in the North, in which freezing civilians await news of the battle for the capture of Fort Donelson in Tennessee, and the scene of the battle itself. On one's first reading Melville's partisan view seems to predominate: the reader hears the reactions of distress or joy of northerners alone and sees only the events on the Union side. But at the end the camera turns from both street and battle to an imaginary scene reminiscent of White-Jacket's vision of the last of the *Neversink* with her guns hoisted out and no "vestige of a fighting thing" left in her, and this ending of "Donelson" calls for a new look at the whole poem, for in it the word *Donelson* (the name of both the fort and the battle) becomes clearly synonymous with "war":

Ah God! may Time with happy haste
Bring wail and triumph to a waste,
    And war be done;
The battle flag-staff fall athwart
The curs'd ravine, and wither; naught
    Be left of trench or gun;
The bastion, let it ebb away,
Washed with the river bed; and Day
    In vain seek Donelson.

Knowing now that in Melville's poetic conception Donelson, fort or battle, is a symbol for war, the rereader can test how often in the poem the word *war* may be substituted for *Donelson:* ice-glazed corpses are sacrifices to Donelson; many an earnest civilian tries to find something in his lot as harrowing as Donelson; the stronghold to be taken is "This winter fort, this stubborn fort, / This castle of the last resort, / This Donelson." Hell is a metaphor for Donelson. After the last stanza other passages, too, take on meanings not seen at first. Looked at in one way they convey a realistic picture of battle; looked at in another way, each is an image of war; or both views come into focus together. "Duels all over 'tween man and man" conveys first the picture of one soldier fighting another at Fort Donelson. Then it becomes the picture of man fighting man "all over" the world and perhaps all over again. Finally, with man and man so close they are "bone to bone," both men become one symbolic man fighting "every where" yet "half unseen." Echoes of fighting nearby become reverberations of wider war. Blood drops showing like clover on a snowy battlefield "like meadows rare" and other images in which death in war contradicts living aspects of nature sharpen the irony of death where fertile life should be. Icy images communicate the idea of death as contrasted with life: "hanging gardens of cold Death" where bloody corpses lie on the slope; boys who, "seeking to crawl in crippled plight, / So stiffened"; and other sights a filmmaker would seize upon. The sting of cold, of fierce "wasps" (sharpshooters), of death nipping boys as cold nips blossoms, all become one sting of Death-in-War.

At the battle's end all is "right"; Fort Donelson is captured. But "horned perplexities" earlier hinted at are still present. There is triumph in the northern street at night, but in the early morning snows women snatch the damp paper tacked on the board, and

> The death-list like a river flows
>> Down the pale sheet,
> And there the whelming waters meet.

The list of Union dead, flowing like a river, suggesting rivers of blood and tears and the eventual washing away of even the names of the dead, is a relatively simple image expressing Melville's feeling about the northern boys killed. More subtle is the larger poetic concept of the meeting of whelming waters, in which we see mingled in Melville's imagination all the dead of this war, of whichever side, and the countless, nameless dead of all wars lost in the river of time.

The dead of North and South meet in Melville's imagination again in "Shiloh." The setting is the scene of a recent battle, a forest field on which there stands a log-built church. The ambiguity of the grammatical role of "mingled" in the quotation below (does it modify "groan" and "prayer" or "foemen"?) mixes the groans, prayers, men, and deaths of both sides. Also shared is the men's sudden enlightenment (undeception) at the moment of death. Swallows are flying over the church

> That echoed to many a parting groan
>> And natural prayer
> Of dying foemen mingled there—
> Foemen at morn, but friends at eve—
>> Fame or country least their care:
> (What like a bullet can undeceive!)

Only the soft sound of the swallows "wheeling still" (the wheeling image implying the seemingly endless repetition of such scenes of death after battles and wars) and the explosive sound of "bullet" break the silence that "Shiloh" establishes to duplicate the stillness of the field where all has been "hushed.".

Modern war and War unite as the theme of "A Utilitarian View of the Monitor's Fight." The "Orient pomp" of War has been laid aside, and to mirror the nakedness Melville strips the poem to its bare idea. He describes the fight of the new ironclads in plain or technical language and draws a conclusion based on a utilitarian view, through which he speaks indirectly and from a dual outlook:

> War shall yet be, and to the end;
>   But war-paint shows the streaks of weather;
> War yet shall be, but warriors
> Are now but operatives; [11] War's made
>   Less grand than Peace,
>   And a singe runs through lace and feather.

To the end of what shall war yet be? Of time? Of man's history? Of the world? Of war itself? The use of a capital letter, so frequent in *Battle-Pieces* to indicate an extreme or inclusive meaning of a word, could have made the phrase read "to the End," that is, to the end, at the minimum, of human existence. On the other hand, the phrase could have read "to its end," pointing to the time—if it ever comes—when humanity puts an end to the institution of war. In neither case would the rhythm have been affected. We can assume that Melville chose to be ambiguous in order to convey both meanings, the second to indicate the intelligent choice humanity should make (the one implied in "War's made less grand than Peace"), and the first to express his emotion as the war continued and intensified with no end in sight.

That the junglelike place in Virginia where fighting went on in May 1863 and May 1864 was called the "Wilderness" naturally stirred Melville's poetic imagination. "The Armies of the Wilderness" is the most complex of the battle scenes and the longest with the exception of "Donelson." The Wilderness in the title is, of course, the actual place; but it is also the wilderness of war and the uncleared wilderness in the heart of man. Similarly, the armies in the title are the armies under Grant that fought in the 1864 Battle of the Wilderness, but also all bodies of men who have ever turned to brute Force to attain either good or evil ends. The ambiguity of the title predicts the complexity of the themes of the poem and reflects Melville's state of mind and heart as he visualized "the fight for the Right" in the actual Wilderness and thought of the continuing horrors in the wilderness of war.

The form Melville gave the poem is another way of hinting at the complexity of the subject—man lost, in every sense, in war's wilderness. What Melville calls his "entangled rhyme" reinforces the sense of humanity's entanglement in war: nineteen stanzas in ordinary type intertwine with nineteen quatrains in italics. The first group describes the action as it unfolds; the second, like the chorus in Sophoclean tragedy, provides the commentary—for instance, the bitter statement that the human species running wild in war is like "jennets let loose / On the Pampas—zebras again." The chorus also raises general questions—for example, the one very much on Melville's mind at the time of the war, "Over and over, again and again / Must the fight for the Right be fought?"

Developed from beginning to end of the scene in the Wilderness are the partisan and the more general feelings. These are not mechanically divided between the passages in ordinary type and those in italics: they wind around each other in each group until in the end they become one as the battle in the pines becomes symbolic of "the maze of war— / . . . / A riddle of death, of which the slain / Sole solvers are." (Since "maze" and "riddle" are in apposition and since the line uses the indefinite instead of the definite article before "riddle of death," I take "death" in this poem, as in "Donelson," to mean death in war and not death as part of the nature of things.)

As in most of *Battle-Pieces*, Melville's profound concern about humanity in relation to war is also the source of what is wonderful in the art of "The Armies in the Wilderness." The partisan language is uniformly bludgeonlike: the southern soldiers, "zealots of the Wrong" were "foully snared by Belial's wily plea" and will be "faithful unto the evil end," while the army under Grant is "the just one" to whom at the end Heaven lends strength, enabling it to strive well and emerge from the Wilderness. In contrast, Melville's passion against war inspires all the conceptions that make "The Armies of the Wilderness" a particularly memorable part of the whole work and a principal example of the oneness of thought and expression that he aimed for in *Battle-Pieces* as a whole.

It is Melville's abhorrence of war that is responsible for the all-inclusive wilderness metaphor and for the merciless realism that is at the same time symbolic. The narrative of the battle conveys war's abortion of life and its distortion of nature's gradual processes. (Aspects of nature that are benign serve Melville's purpose in this poem.) The most outstanding example is the chilling moment in which war's travesty of life is suddenly seen in a stunning image. Northern soldiers are in pursuit of the enemy through woods where fighting took place the year before (the emphasis is mine):

> In glades they meet skull after skull
>   Where pine-cones lay—the rusted gun,
> Green shoes full of bones, the mouldering coat
>   *And cuddled-up skeleton.*

Cuddled is a warm word, connoting comfort and love. One's image of a cuddled-up figure is likely to be that of a baby or fetus. Alone, "cuddled-up" is capable of conveying to one's own flesh and bones the physical sensation of being curled up, cared for, or consoled. But what we see are the bones of a soldier who died in an earlier battle. Instead of the abandon of youth (marching "lustily" in "Ball's Bluff" and in "Bacchic glee" in "The March into Virginia"), an abandoned, fleshless body lies wasted. What should be and what is are discordant; even the sound of "cuddled-up skeleton" is cacophonous. The one image compresses the soldier's life into a single instant: his growth in the womb, birth, childhood, youth, and death are all seen in a rapid photographic shot. The soldier's identity is lost. He is any unknown soldier. His clothes show no Union or Confederate colors: [12] his shoes are green with what must be mold; his moldering coat must also be green, not blue or gray. All the ironic overtones of two short lines combine to ask, "Was man born for such a death?"

Strange juxtapositions of man and Nature, symbolic contrasts, and odd uses of words with multiple and often contradictory meanings also contribute to the impression of war's mockery of what we think of as the normal process of childhood, youth, gradual aging, and only then death. The headstone of a grave is used as a hearthstone on which water is "bubbling" for punch for bubbling young singers soon to die; they are "beating time" with their swords to "rollicking staves," Melville's manipulation of words implying that they are beating out, although they don't think about it, the time left before the battle in which they may die, which is just being staved off for a short lively while. Northern soldiers through their glass see the enemy playing baseball, and "They could have joined them in their sport / But for the vale's deep rent." Melville, who wrote of grotesque war games in *Mardi*, conveys through "sport" and "the vale's deep rent" (twin of the "curs'd ravine" in "Donelson") that the divided sides will all too soon rejoin each other in the "sport" of war. Nuts that cannot grow again on massacred trees, birds evicted from those trees, and boys who will never go nutting again are brought together in an effective strange combination. The grass shimmers, not in the sun, but in the bayonets' sheen. Dead faces are "white as pebbles in a well," tossed, that is, as if they were pebbles, into a well that may be meant as a symbol of time.

Bitter as Melville is about man's continued reenactment of the crime of Cain, to whom he refers here, as in many other works,[13] he does not say that humans are by nature without the potentiality of living in peace. The chorus comments on Grant:

> *Were men but strong and wise,*
> *Honest as Grant, and calm,*
> *War would be left to the red and black ants,*
> *And the happy world disarm.*

But men generally do not possess this combination of qualities, and even Grant, whose heart is "as calm / As the cyclone's core," has had to nurse the scheme that now "bursts into act—into war." Will humanity ever emerge from the Wilderness of war, never to return? Does the poem finally give a negative or affirmative answer? The ending is:

> None can narrate that strife in the pines,
>   A seal is on it—Sabaean lore!
> Obscure as the wood, the entangled rhyme

But hints at the maze of war—
Vivid glimpses or livid through peopled gloom,
    And fires which creep and char—
A riddle of death, of which the slain
        Sole solvers are.

Long they withhold the roll
    Of the shroudless dead. It is right;
Not yet can we bear the flare
    Of the funeral light.

On the one hand, since the slain are the "sole" solvers, the poem seems to say that the living will never solve the riddle of death in war, a negative answer that would concur with those passages in which men are associated with zebras and red or black ants. On the other hand, the present tense in "Sole solvers are" is ambiguous. It may mean "always"; it may mean "now." That the slain now are the sole solvers would harmonize with what Melville says about the living: *"Not yet* can we bear the flare." Glimpses, some "vivid," of the maze of war, are available. The poem shares them. Besides, Melville does not use the word *glare*, a word used elsewhere in *Battle-Pieces*, but *flare*, one meaning of which is a light that can be borne for shared illumination. That the chorus has the last word indicates yet again that the conception of the Civil War as tragedy underlies this poem to the end, and in tragedy, while enlightenment in most cases comes to the hero just before he or she dies, the survivors, as the drama ends, also look to the future with some new understanding of life, its dangers, and human causes of suffering. The last line of the poem leaves us on the way to such a moment, the paradoxical phrase "funeral light" hinting at the illumination the death of others can bring to the living. Yet, although it is made possible that if "not yet" then later the survivors will be able to understand more, the ending is not an affirmative answer about whether man will ever emerge for good from the maze of war. As always in *Battle-Pieces*, the question is asked, not answered. So the ending is a riddle, as Melville's idea about form as an expression of theme demands. The poem as a whole is a wilderness / maze / riddle, with its interlacing stanzas (its "entangled rhyme") continuing to the very end, in order that "The Armies of the Wilderness" will continue to ask its large question of the reader.

Reminders that "Right" in *Battle-Pieces* means, above all, the end of slavery, reappear in the drama in the second half of the second act. In "The Swamp Angel," Michael, who had been the "white man's seraph," joins the symbolic "coal-black Angel" whose messengers are cannon shells crumbling the walls of Charleston; these cause "farther walls" to fall, "farther portals," the repetition suggesting that not only are actual walls and gates falling but also the walls of slavery. Another reminder is the variation of the refrain in "The March to the Sea" after the stanza tells us that the banners of Sherman's army "The slaves by thousands drew, / And they marched beside the drumming, / And they joined the armies blue":

> It was glorious glad marching,
> For every man was free.

Conflict between commitment to the just war and antipathy to War continues until the end of the middle act—until, that is, the war is over. "The Fall of Richmond" rejoices at the victory but mourns the "weary years and woeful wars, / And armies in the grave." In "The Surrender at Appomattox" a happy omen is seen in "Freedom's larger play," but the "loud joy-gun, whose thunders run / By sea-shore, streams, and lakes," is an indirect reminder of the years of war guns thundering over the country, the composite picture of which recalls the similar one in "Misgivings," when the storm of war is beginning. The act ends with three closely related poems that form a dramatic unit. The rainbow sparkles at last over the waterfall in "A Canticle," but the Giant of the Pool heaves his head upward, threatening the rainbow of peace, the biblical symbol of God's promise to humanity. The poem, though seemingly a prayer, signifies that we cannot be sure the "Lord of hosts victorious" will or can fulfill a beautiful "end designed" and that nothing is ever secure for all time. Then, as if to emphasize that negative possibilities always exist, "The Martyr" tells of the assassination of Lincoln on Good Friday (only five days after the surrender at Appomattox). It hints at possible tragic consequences of what Melville makes more than an individual crime by speaking in the plural of "parricides," by alluding to the Christ story and to the story of Abraham, and by making heaven call on the new president to avenge the crime "in righteousness." Immediately after "The Martyr," in which the assassination seems like both the last shot of the war and the possible start of another, the last poem of the act, "The Coming Storm," whose title is the name of a painting by S. R. Gifford, fuses thoughts of the war, of the assassination, and of tragedy. Once more actual circumstances lend a battle-piece its imagery. Melville had seen the painting just after the assassination, at a National Academy exhibition in New York; its subject, a coming storm, had long been his image for the war arising from slavery; and the owner of the painting was Edwin Booth, famous actor in Shakespearean tragedy and brother of the assassin. Melville imagines Edwin Booth to have bought the painting with a dim feeling that it presaged a disaster. The poem conveys that so terrible a fate as war or knowledge of a brother's crime can be no "utter surprise" to one who reaches "Shakespeare's core," the knowledge that tragedy may always be forming, like the storm; that it can be forefelt; and that human beings are capable of destruction (like the assassination and the war) as well as of creation (like Booth's or Gifford's or Shakespeare's art.)

The last act brings the enlargement of vision that comes at the end of tragedy. "The Apparition: (A Retrospect)" is Melville's backward look at the war, followed by a generalization and a caveat:

> CONVULSIONS came; and, where the field
>   Long slept in pastoral green,
> A goblin-mountain was upheaved
> (Sure the scared sense was all deceived),
>   Marl-glen and slag-ravine.
>
> The unreserve of Ill was there,
>   The clinkers in her last retreat;
> But, ere the eye could take it in,

Or mind could comprehension win,
   It sunk!—and at our feet.

So, then, Solidity's a crust—
   The core of fire below;
All may go well for many a year,
But who can think without a fear
   Of horrors that happen so?

As in "Dupont's Round Fight," the significance of "so" (here the climactic last word of the poem) needs special attention, in order to avoid the interpretation that the poem contradicts, namely, that it offers insight into evil as the ultimate reality responsible for disasters that "inexplicably"burst forth and that the Civil War is of negligible significance in the poem: "Curiously, and quite significantly," to one interpreter, "the Civil War is not even mentioned in this poem." [14] An examination of this "Retrospect" to see what "so" points to reveals that the evil is human and not incomprehensible, even though it was not generally comprehended and that the volcanic upheaval is, of course, the war. The first two stanzas are a backward look at the national convulsion and also at the opening poems of *Battle-Pieces,* which were the forewarnings of it. The "pastoral green" recalls the soon-to-be destroyed "green" on which John Brown's shadow lengthens; "The unreserve of Ill" harks back to "my country's ills" and "man's foulest crime"; and the image sustained throughout "The Apparition," of accumulating "Ill" leading to an outburst, is a reminder of the tempest of war "bursting from the waste of Time" in "Misgivings," the storms behind the one we feel in the same poem, and the communicated sense of time passing while slavery continues in "The Portent." But let us look at the poem apart from these reminders.

The catastrophe described in the first two stanzas is a metaphor first of the sudden upheaval that was the war and then of the reestablishment of seeming solidity as the war ended. Convulsions come to a green field (America) that long "slept," *sleeping,* in the context, implying the dormancy of a volcano and the unawareness of people. The field is misshaped into a grotesque mountain of cindery lava replacing fertile soil. The nature of the phenomenon and what caused it is unclear to the "scared sense," though the full flow of the lava (the "Ill" previously restrained underground where it built up the heat leading to the eruption) is now exposed to view. (*Apparition* denotes the act of becoming visible.) But "the eye" and "mind" (physical and mental perception) are unable to take in, though the plain sight is before them, that "Ill" long boiling under the surface was the origin of the eruption. Then (when, presumably, the lava that is still flowing pulls back below the ground) the mountain sinks, and the apparition is over. Again nothing dangerous is visible.

Since neither physical nor mental perception is adequate for understanding, the poet must awaken imagination. The first two lines of the last stanza attempt to make visible to the inner eye the generalization of the experience, namely, that seeming "Solidity" can, like the earth's surface, be broken. Under Solidity's crust potentially dangerous processes go on; by implication, beneath a country's surface there may be buried "Ill" whose heat is building up. What remains of "Ill" after the Civil War—for slavery was not the only one of the "country's ills"—may be storing up new heat capable of causing future violence. (The "Supplement" asks, "In the recent convulsion has the crater but shifted?") [15] The last three lines address the country. Like "Kubla Khan" they seem to say, "Beware! Beware!" America should think with fear of horrors that happen "so." Even though in "The Apparition" a natural phenomenon provided Melville with his metaphor, his subject is not Nature. What motivated his imagination was concern for the future fate of the country, beloved at this time, in spite of everything wrong with it.

The tragedy ends with "America," which is both a retrospect and a look ahead. Four tableaulike scenes in which America appears in human form tell the story of the nation from its founding to the end of the Civil War. In the first, she is a young mother folding her children to her "exulting" heart; Melville must have had the idea of tragic hubris in mind. In the second stanza a tempest mingles with the fray of her children, and she stands stricken. In the third she falls into what at first looks like death to a "watcher," who then sees that it is a nightmare-filled sleep and that the contortions of her face express the "terror" of what she sees. Her vision bares earth's foundation, including Gorgon (kin of "Ill" and "core of fire") in her hidden underground place. The watcher finds it "a thing of fear to see / So foul a dream upon so fair a face, / And the dreamer lying in that starry shroud." The pairing of "fair" and "foul" as in *Macbeth* (and "Misgivings") reminds us again of tragic drama. So does the concept of the "watcher" (viewer, audience) and the "terror" the watcher of tragic drama vicariously feels. With this reminder we are prepared for the last scene in the historic tragedy in which enlightenment comes, though "mysteries dimly sealed," to use Melville's phrase in "Donelson," remain.

The first half of the last stanza contains echoes of the end of the choral drama in verse generally thought to have the effect of tragedy. In his conclusion of *Samson Agonistes* Milton speaks of "true experience from this great event," of "peace," and of "calm of mind, all passion spent." Melville says of America:

> But from the trance she sudden broke—
> The trance, or death into promoted life;
> At her feet a shivered yoke,
> And in her aspect turned to heaven
> No trace of passion or of strife—
> A clear calm look. It spake of pain,
> But such as purifies from stain.

Now America is the image of growth, enlightenment, purification, and release from tension after the experience of tragic conflict and suffering. The fair and not the foul possibilities of the future are brought to the viewer's mind. America has arisen from a kind of death into "promoted life." The yoke of slavery has been broken by violence; America is purified of the stain of crime and blood. In what follows, she is "matured," with new knowledge and a sense of Law and control. In contrast to the crime-linked hope in "Misgivings," her hope is now "wise." The shadow (image of associated slavery and violence in *Mardi*, *Benito Cereno*, and earlier poems in *Battle-Pieces*) has been "chased by light"—by enlightenment. *But*, in accordance with Melville's feeling about "Shakespeare's core"—

the knowledge that nothing is sure about the future and that new tragic events may be enacted—America is left, in the last line of the drama, "on the crag." With that picture of 1865 America on a bare and lonely height to remain in the inner eye of the "watcher," Melville brings down the curtain in the form of a blank page separating the historic tragedy from the pieces not included in it but grouped instead as "Verses Inscriptive and Memorial."

Written with "few exceptions" [16] in the time between the fall of Richmond in April 1865, when Melville's tension about the war was eased, and the submission of the volume to Harper & Brothers prior to its publication in the summer of 1866, the poems in the drama, however varied in mood, are the work of an imagination that had an overview of the war and the nation's history. The poems Melville chose for *Battle-Pieces* are indeed pieces of a large conception. In interpreting the thought and feeling of individual poems, their images should be looked at not only in the particular context but in relation to those kindred images that move from "The Portent" through "America." Of these Melville's conception of the Civil War as the historic tragedy of the country, explicit in the "Supplement" and implicit in the drama, is the encompassing nourishing image of *Battle-Pieces*.

Notes

1. Herman Melville, *Battle-Pieces,* ed. Sidney Kaplan (Gainesville, Fla.: Scholars' Facsimiles & Reprints, 1960).
2. In his own copy of the book Melville changed "terrible" to "great."
3. From Melville's prefatory note.
4. William H. Shurr, *The Mystery of Iniquity* (Lexington: The University Press of Kentucky, 1972), p. 43.
5. "On the Slain Collegians," l. 28.
6. *Macbeth,* I, v. 59.
7. Hennig Cohen implies that the name Brown suggested to Melville the brown of devastation. This is only one of countless ideas about the origins of images in the poems and about related images elsewhere in Melville in Cohen's "Introduction" and notes to *Battle-Pieces* (New York: Thomas Yoseloff, 1964). Some of the most exciting of these ideas concern Melville's interest in visual art and the probable influence of certain paintings and pieces of sculpture on poems in *Battle-Pieces*. The edition itself is a work of visual art. It distributes Civil War drawings by Alfred and William Waud throughout the pages of

poetry, and pictures of paintings owned or seen by Melville that must have influenced the poetry illustrate the notes.

8. Merton M. Sealts, *Melville's Reading* (Madison: Univ. of Wisconsin Press, 1966), entries 147 and 332.

9. Shurr, p. 26.

10. Robert Penn Warren, *Selected Poems of Herman Melville* (New York: Random House, 1970), p. 14.

11. The conception of sailors on a warship as "operatives" did not originate in Melville's mind in connection with the new ironclads. In *Israel Potter* the men of the *Serapis* work at the row of guns "as Lowell girls the rows of looms in a cotton factory."

12. The poetic concept of a skeleton giving no indication of a man's origin plays an important part in *Benito Cereno*.

13. In *Mardi* the primal crime is Cain's killing of his brother man; in *Billy Budd* virtues "out of keeping" with modern custom and civilization seem transmitted from a period prior to Cain's city; and in "On the Slain Collegians" in *Battle-Pieces* the idea of heroism or duty may be masks of Cain.

14. Shurr, p. 43.

15. *Battle-Pieces,* p. 268. The "Supplement" is, in relation to slavery, a presentation in prose of ideas that animate the poetry, but in relation to Reconstruction it is, as I read it, Melville's one real failure of historical and poetic imagination. My analysis of "The Supplement" is the second half of my essay, "Melville and the Civil War," in *New Letters,* 40 (Winter 1973), 99–117.

16. *Battle-Pieces,* prefatory note.

9.

Billy Budd and Melville's Philosophy of War and Peace

Billy Budd, Sailor [1] concentrates Melville's philosophy of war and lifts it to its highest point of development. Its themes are recapitulations and extensions of those he had many times developed, and its poetic conceptions are the offspring of earlier ones that had embodied his ideas concerning the "greatest of evils." [2] Even the manuscript record of his revision gives evidence of his need to express as perfectly as possible his thinking about the ill that had been at the center of his imagination for almost half a century [3] and his vision of the "civilized" and "Christian" world in which the essence of war and evil is one. His reluctance to finish is understandable. In his seventies he could not count on another chance to set forth so scrupulously his view of the man-of-war world as a parody of the Christianity it feigns or to awaken other imaginations to "holier" [4] values than those civilized man had lived by.

The view of *Billy Budd* as the final stage in the development of Melville's philosophy of war embraces both the work's abhorrence of war and the war machine (the feeling ignored by those who, in the classical argument about *Billy Budd*, see it as a "testament of acceptance") and its genuinely affirmative, non-ironic, and luminous aspects (the qualities set aside by those who see it in its total-

160

ity as irony, rejection, or darkness alone). Along with Melville's continued rejection of the world of war there is in *Billy Budd* a new affirmation that within that world's most cruel contradictions lies the potentiality of its metamorphosis.

It is now generally believed that *Billy Budd, Sailor* was originally intended for inclusion in *John Marr and Other Sailors* since an early draft of the ballad with which the story ends goes back to 1886 when other poems with short prose introductions in the collection were being composed.[5] But as one can see from the Hayford and Sealts genetic text, which traces the changes Melville made during the years of *Billy Budd*'s composition, Melville sensed early the potentialities that a development of the basic situation—the execution of a sailor in wartime—could have. It could present an unforgettable picture of the essential nature of the world of war and, at the same time, suggest its complexities, which the imagination of man must penetrate. The revisions move steadily in the direction of realizing these potentialities ever more fully,[6] until in the end *Billy Budd* becomes a work to remain in the reader's memory as simultaneously one of the most simple of fictional works—in terms of story—and one of the most complex in terms of what is implied by the art with which the story is presented.

By the time of his last work Melville was so experienced a poet and narrator that he could rely solely on poetic conceptions integrated into narrative to carry his ideas. For this reason it is possible to consider all main aspects of the work in the course of recalling the story.

What happens in *Billy Budd,* with the exception of what takes place within the psyche of the crew, is what Melville had all along demonstrated must necessarily happen—what is, in that sense, fated—in the "present civilisation of the world." [7] Impressed from the English merchant ship *Rights-of-Man* [8] to serve the king on the battleship *Bellipotent* in 1797, the year of the Great Mutiny during the Napoleonic wars, Billy is almost literally *White-Jacket*'s sailor "shorn of all rights" (lxxii, 301). Young and of considerable physical and personal beauty, like Melville's typical "Handsome Sailor" in aspect though not like him a "spokesman" (44), called "peacemaker" and "jewel" by the merchantman's captain (47), and "flower of the flock" and a "beauty" by the lieutenant who carries him off (48), he is from the first the symbol of the good and beauty "out of keeping" (53) and doomed in the world of war. He is, at the same time, representative of sailors as a class, as the title *Billy Budd, Sailor* conveys. The words of John Marr, describing seamen generally, apply to him: "Taking things as fated merely, / Child-like through the world ye spanned; / Nor holding unto life too dearly, / . . . Barbarians of man's simpler nature, / Unworldly servers of the world." [9] He is shortly seen to represent also the jewel and flower of youth sacrificed to war, like the soldiers in *Battle-Pieces* "nipped like blossoms," [10] willing children sent through fire as sacrifices to a false god, fated to die because an older generation has failed to rectify wrongs that lead to war. In either aspect— representative or outstanding—he incorporates *White-Jacket*'s conception of a sailor as the "image of his Creator" (xxxiv, 142).

Billy accepts his impressment without complaint. Like the crew of the *Pequod* and all but a few sailors on the *Neversink*, he is incapable of saying *no* to anyone in authority, or indeed of speaking at all when he most needs speech to defend himself. His "imperfection" is made concrete in an actual "defect," a tongue-tie, or "more or less of a stutter or even worse" (53). The reverse of this "organic hesitancy"—the ability to speak up to authority—is possessed by no one in *Billy Budd,* but the dedication to Jack Chase, whose outstanding quality in *White-Jacket* had been his willingness to be a spokesman, points up the contrast. There is no one resembling him on the *Bellipotent,* a rereading of the dedication after the novel is read will remind one—no independent spirit to speak up firmly for Billy.

The day after Billy's impressment the *Bellipotent*'s crew must witness an admonitory flogging.[11] The young sailor, now a foretop-man, vows never to do anything to bring down on himself such a punishment or even a reproof. But while he never does, and while his simple virtue, friendliness, and good looks make him well liked by the crew, these very qualities arouse a "peculiar" (73) hostility in Claggart, the master-at-arms, a functionary "peculiar" to battle-ships. Billy's goodness calls forth a natural antipathy in Claggart; the devil associated in Melville's imagination with war resides in Claggart as once before in Bland, the master-at-arms in *White-Jacket,* and again is inevitably hostile to all good. What Melville stresses in both masters-at-arms is their function. The diabolical power of each derives from his position, given him by the war machine. Claggart's "place" puts "converging wires of underground influence" under his control (67). The Navy "charges" him with his police duties so that he can preserve its "order" (64, 93). He lives in "offical seclusion" from the light (64). The words *function* and *functionary* are regularly used in relation to him. Since his qualities are what the navy needs in a master-at-arms, it has advanced him rapidly to his post; and, as with Bland, it defends him—posthumously in his case—even when his evil is exposed. His mystery—something to be probed—is social in its significance and consequences, not something so remote, so emptily abstract and supernatural that one must abandon all attempts to understand it and must accept it as man's fate. The depravity Claggart stands for is encouraged by the values that dominate the world: "Civilization, especially if of the austerer sort, is auspicious to it. It folds itself in the mantle of respectability" (75).

Melville accents the mutually exclusive character of the values of war and peace, for which Claggart and Billy stand, in an unusual spatial way, in terms of "the juxtaposition of dissimilar personalities" (74); the "mutually confronting visages" of the master-at-arms and the young sailor (98); and their eventual assignment to "opposite" compartments (101). Billy is associated with the sunlight; the master-at-arms, with the contrasting space, the shade. They are "essential right and wrong," which in the "jugglery of circumstances" attending war are interchanged (103). For what is evil for man is war's good; what is good for mankind is that for which war has no place.

An old Danish sailor's thoughts present the question to which the book responds. Seeing in Billy—"Baby," as he calls him—something "in contrast" with the warship's "environment" and "oddly incongruous" with it, he wonders what will befall such a nature in such a world (70). He warns Billy that Claggart is down on him, but just as Claggart is powerless to contain any good, so Billy is unable to take in the evil of the master-at-arms.

At a moment when the *Bellipotent* is on detached service from the fleet, Claggart seeks an interview with Captain Vere. He accuses Billy of plotting mutiny, a charge well calculated to create fear at that moment, but one Vere cannot credit in the case of the young sailor. Called in to face the accusation, Billy is speechless with horror, his "impotence" noted by the captain (99). Claggart's eyes as he confronts Billy lose their human expression. His first glance is that of a serpent, his last that of a torpedo fish, Melville again associating the devil, as represented by the serpent, with war, as implied by the torpedo. Unable to use his tongue, Billy can express himself against Claggart only with a blow, which strikes the master-at-arms in the forehead, and the body falls dead.

Vere's instantaneous utterance, "Fated boy" (99), unconsciously pronounces Billy's doom. His response is the result of conditioning so strong that his verdict has the force of an instinct. The moment sets forth dramatically what was put forward as exposition in *White-Jacket* in regard to the power which a man-of-war captain's long-instilled prejudices and training have over his thought (lv, 232). So thoroughly has Vere been dedicated to the ritual of war that to him it seems Fate. He covers and then uncovers his face, the "father in him, manifested towards Billy thus far in the scene . . . replaced by the military disciplinarian" (100). This is a gentler version, but an imaginatively related version, nonetheless, of the two faces of the *Neversink*'s captain, a fatherly one for special occasions and an uncompromising judge's face when he condemns a man to be flogged. The two faces cannot coincide. The face of the military disciplinarian in Vere must take the place of that of the father.

Vere at this point has to make his conscious choice between God's will and that of Mars. He is not in any degree unclear about the nature of that choice; in his mind Claggart has been struck dead by an "angel of God." But neither is he for a moment undecided about his verdict: "Yet the angel must hang" (101). For, as Melville will make increasingly clear, the God whom Vere has been trained to worship is Mars; his religion is war; his thoughts and acts are conditioned by the ritual patterns of warmaking. So he silences that part of himself which recognizes God in Billy; he is, in effect, knowingly striking at God when he decides to sacrifice God's angel. Melville shows him self-alienated to the extreme. Vere does feel sympathy, even deep love for Billy, but "a true military officer is in one particular like a true monk. Not with more of self-abnegation will the latter keep his vows of monastic obedience than the former his allegiance to martial duty" (104). The comparison extrapolates the one in *Clarel* in which an imagined warship is a grim abbey afloat on the ocean, its discipline cenobite and dumb, its deep galleries "cloisters of the god of war." [12] Indeed, as far back as *White-Jacket,* officers had been "priests of Mars" (xlix, 209) and an English fighting frigate's tall mainmast had terminated, ironically, "like a steepled cathedral, in the bannered cross of the religion of peace" (lxv, 268). Throughout *Billy Budd* the contrast between the religion of war and "the religion of Peace" is evoked, largely by church images—an altar, a place of sanctuary, confessionals or side chapels, sacraments, covenants, and ceremonial forms—until the *Bellipotent* becomes, in effect, a cathedral dedicated to War. Billy is an offering Vere makes to Mars, an offering not demanded by law or ethics or even military necessity (Melville plainly eliminating these as Vere's felt motivations) but by his own obsession.

Vere's inner compulsion, like Ahab's, drives him so "steadfastly" on (113) that he cannot delay. As he prepares to make his sacrifice, he is so strangely excited that the surgeon who has been called in to attend to the corpse wonders whether he is sane (101). The question thus raised about Vere's sanity is a symbolic one, the concrete poetic expression of Melville's long conception of war as the "madness" in men. A significant subsidiary question is presented as well: Does Vere's strange behavior indicate a sudden aberration, a "transient excitement" brought about by the unusual circumstances? Vere's devotion to war—his "madness"—is not sudden; it is his constant state of mind. But the peculiar circumstances of Billy's killing of Claggart bring his obsession into sharper focus.

Instead of waiting to submit Billy's case to the admiral when they rejoin the fleet, as the other officers think should be done, Vere sets up the form, though not the substance, of a trial, carefully selecting the members of his court. He conducts the proceedings in extreme secrecy. The naval court-martial that *White-Jacket* condemns as a "Star Chamber indeed!" and compares with the Spanish Inquisition (lxxii, 302) here resembles those palace tragedies that occurred in the capital founded by the czar of Russia, "Peter the Barbarian" (103).

The first part of the trial, which establishes the facts and at which Billy is present, presents in dramatic form ideas set forth in *White-Jacket,* Billy being the representative "plebian topman, without a jury . . . judicially naked at the bar" (lxxii, 303), and Vere the captain clothed with unlimited, arbitrary powers. To Billy, who cannot say *no* to anyone in power, a foundling child who wants to be liked and who fears to call forth even a reproof, Vere, the King's aristocratic "envoy" (60), is someone he could certainly never gainsay. His statement, "I have eaten the King's bread and I am true to the King" (106), recalls the unquestioning obedience exacted in return for food in *Moby-Dick*'s cabin-table scene in which men waiting to be served by Ahab are as little children humble before the captain, whose war they will serve without question, and even Starbuck, the chief mate, receives his meat as though receiving alms.[13] Billy's words, suggesting as they do a sacrament and a covenant, contribute to a contrast between the bargain between men and kings who give them food so that they may feed upon them and the covenant between man and God by which man will live according to the ethical standards represented by God. One realizes at this point why Melville had earlier made Vere refer to Billy as, in "naval parlance," a "King's bargain" (95).

Although Billy symbolizes what is essentially good, he has the weakness of the sailors he represents: his silence gives consent to war's demands. When he grasps what Vere has in mind for him, he acquiesces to the decision as to Fate. His silence—like that of all the others on the *Bellipotent,* including the silence of Vere's humane part—is an accessory of war, partaking of its evil. Thus, an earlier remark about Billy, unexplained at the time, is clarified, namely, that his vocal flaw shows that "the arch interferer, the envious marplot of Eden, still has more or less to do with every human consignment to this planet of Earth" (53).

After Billy is sent back to the compartment opposite the one where Claggart's body is, the second part of the trial (109–14), the arrival at a joint verdict, begins. Vere asks the question he knows to be in the officers' minds: "How can we adjudge to summary and shameful death a fellow creature innocent before God, and whom we feel to be so?—Does that state it aright? You sign sad assent. Well, I too feel that, the full force of that. It is Nature." But he urges the court to remember that their allegiance has been sworn to the king, not to Nature. And now, as in his most subtle earlier fiction, Melville speaks through another, saying in part what that character says but in essence and in total intention something far different; it is the technique used with special artistry in the case of Captain Delano in *Benito Cereno* and of Judge Hall in *The Confidence-Man*. Speaking through Vere, Melville espouses the reverse of the religion for which Vere proselytizes. The captain addresses to the court what could stand alone in another context as an eloquent speech against war. He does not intend it so; Melville, however, does, conveying obliquely that war itself is the "Great Mutiny" against God, striking at "essential right." It is Vere, not Melville, who rules out "moral scruple" in favor of that strength in war, that bellipotence, which to him is "paramount." Through Vere's speech to the court Melville reveals the absence of morality in war and shows himself prophetically sensitive to a question whose centrality would not be generally clear until well into the twentieth century, the question of individual conscience and responsibility in time of war. Vere asks:

> suppose condemnation to follow these present proceedings. Would it be so much we ourselves that would condemn as it would be martial law operating through us? For that law and the rigor of it, we are not responsible. Our vowed responsibility is in this: That however pitilessly that law may operate in any instances, we nevertheless adhere to it and administer it. (110–11)

He urges that warm hearts not betray heads that should be cool, that in war the heart, "the feminine in man," must be ruled out. As for conscience, "tell me whether or not, occupying the position we do, private conscience should not yield to that imperial one formulated in the code under which alone we officially proceed" (111).

When one member of the court-martial pleads that Billy intended neither mutiny nor homicide, he replies:

before a court less arbitrary and more merciful than a martial
one, that plea would largely extenuate. At the Last Assizes it
shall acquit. But how here? We proceed under the law of the
Mutiny Act. In feature no child can resemble his father more
than that Act resembles in spirit the thing from which it derives—War. (111–12).

Yet to the letter of that law Vere works to convert the court; the
Mutiny Act is, in the words of *White-Jacket* about the Articles of
War, his "gospel" (lxx, 292).

To guarantee their going along with his "prejudgment" (108),
Vere concludes with an appeal to the officers' sense of fear, his
argument being that the crew, learning of Billy's deed and seeing
him continue alive, will believe the *Bellipotent*'s officers weak and
may mutiny against them. This appeal prevails. In any event,
Vere's subordinates are, like Billy, "without the faculty, hardly . . .
the inclination to gainsay" him (113). So Billy is sentenced to be
hanged at the yardarm at dawn. Vere takes upon himself the burden of telling him privately "the finding of the court" (114), knowing Billy will feel for him (113).

The narrator gives no account of the interview, only a conjecture
that Vere in the end may have developed the passion sometimes
"latent" under a stoical exterior: "The austere devotee of military
duty, letting himself melt back into what remains primeval in our
formalized humanity, may in end have have caught Billy to his
heart, even as Abraham may have caught young Isaac on the brink
of resolutely offering him up in obedience to the exacting behest"
(115). The narrator sees a resemblance between the two situations,
the one biblical, the other military, in order that Melville may
accent the contrast between the God who created man and the god
of war who would destroy him. For God in the story of Isaac and
Abraham does not in the end exact the sacrifice. In the history of
the ancient Jews, as told by those who composed the Old Testament, the Abraham-Isaac story signifies the first recorded repudia-
tion of the tradition of human sacrifice. It is God's final behest that
Isaac should live and that Abraham's seed should multiply
through him. But Vere's internal behest condemns Billy, and the
tradition of human sacrifice on the altar of war goes on.

Nevertheless Vere does suffer, and intensely; it is one of the most important ideas in the work that all suffer from war. The senior lieutenant sees Vere leave the compartment, and "the face he beheld, for the moment one expressive of the agony of the strong, was to that officer, though a man of fifty, a startling revelation" (115). His is the agony of a martyr to an inhumane religion. By turning from Billy, as Ahab does from Pip, Vere turns from his own humanity, sacrificing to war his capacity for love, for "fatherhood." All that will seem to remain of him from this moment on is his military function. He has adhered to his choice between the values represented by Claggart and by Billy, sacrificing Billy and what he represents and, in effect, upholding what Claggart stands for. And suddenly we know why it was said earlier of Claggart's depravity that civilization, "especially if of the austerer sort" (more denying of its heart), is auspicious to it.

Underlining the reversal of human values in war, Melville has Claggart prepared for burial "with every funeral honor properly belonging to his naval grade" (117), while Billy lies on the upper deck awaiting an ignominious death. Billy's significance as the good and beauty sacrificed to war is represented as if in a painting. Since all of *Billy Budd* is only some eighty pages, the two-page painting [14] of the young sailor (118–20) in a bay formed by the regular spacing of the guns must have been of extreme symbolic importance to Melville. Billy lies between two guns "as nipped in the vice of fate." The guns painted black and the heavy hempen breechings tarred the same color seem to wear the livery of undertakers. "In contrast with the funereal hue of these surroundings," Billy lies in his soiled white sailor's apparel, which glimmers in the obscure light. "In effect he is already in his shroud." Worked into the painting is the basic contrast between the ignored values of Christianity and the values actually held sacred in modern civilization.

> Over him but scarce illuminating him, two battle lanterns swing from two massive beams of the deck above. Fed with the oil supplied by the war contractors (whose gains, honest or otherwise, are in every land an anticipated portion of the harvest of death), with flickering splashes of dirty yellow light

they pollute the pale moonshine all but ineffectually strug-
gling in obstructed flecks through the open ports from which
the tampioned cannon protrude. Other lanterns at intervals
serve but to bring out somewhat the obscurer bays which, like
small confessionals or side-chapels in a cathedral, branch from
the long dim-vistaed broad aisle between the two batteries of
that covered tier.

With something of the look of a slumbering child in the cradle, a
serene light coming and going on his face as he dreams, Billy is a
picture of innocence, beauty, and peace doomed in the world of
war.

The chaplain who comes to talk to Billy finds him asleep in a
peace that transcends any consolation he has to offer. This chaplain, also an accessory of war, is gentler than the one in *White-
Jacket* (xxxviii), but his role, in essence, is the same; indeed it is
more fully developed and strongly stated. Melville stresses his function and the contrast between the religion he preaches and the one
he serves.

> Bluntly put, a chaplain is the minister of the Prince of
> Peace serving in the host of the God of War—Mars. As such,
> he is as incongruous as a musket would be on the altar at
> Christmas. Why, then, is he there? Because he indirectly sub-
> serves the purpose attested by the cannon; because too he
> lends the sanction of the religion of the meek to that which
> practically is the abrogation of everything but brute Force.
> (122)

The luminous moonlit night passes away, but "like the prophet
in the chariot disappearing in heaven and dropping his mantle to
Elisha," it transfers its pale robe "to the breaking day" and a faint
light rises slowly in the East (122). With this association with
Elijah and the transfer of his mantle to suggest a progression to a
brighter future day, the early phrase, "the mantle of respectability," to signify the cloak which civilization lends to Claggartlike
depravity (75) seems to have been meticulously worded to light the

difference when this moment would appear. For the transfer of Elijah's mantle to Elisha and the slowly rising light in the East imply an advance to a day when men will no longer worship false gods (the baals from whose designation the name Beelzebub for the devil derives) and will fulfill their latent "God-given" humanity.[15] This prophecy, with the believable reality upon which Melville will base it, is the source of the luminescence that, despite the painful events to come, will irradiate the remainder of the work.

At four in the morning silver whistles summon all hands on deck to witness punishment. The crew's silence, like Billy's, gives consent. Only at the moment of his death does Billy's frozen speech become fluid, touching something deep within the crew. But the greater eloquence is Melville's as he speaks through the young sailor and the scene of his execution (123–28). His art makes the spectacle "admonitory" for the reader, as for the crew, in another sense entirely from the one Vere intends. Billy stands facing aft.

> At the penultimate moment, his words, his only ones, words wholly unobstructed in the utterance, were these: "God bless Captain Vere!" Syllables so unanticipated coming from one with the ignominious hemp about his neck—a conventional felon's benediction directed aft towards the quarters of honor; syllables too delivered in the clear melody of a singing bird on the point of launching from the twig—had a phenomenal effect, not unenhanced by the rare personal beauty of the young sailor, spiritualized now through late experiences so poignantly profound.
>
> Without volition, as it were, as if indeed the ship's populace were but the vehicles of some vocal current electric, with one voice from alow and aloft came a resonant sympathetic echo: "God bless Captain Vere!" And yet at that instant Billy alone must have been in their hearts, even as in their eyes.
>
> At the pronounced words and the spontaneous echo that voluminously rebounded them, Captain Vere, either through stoic self-control or a sort of momentary paralysis induced by emotional shock, stood rigidly erect as a musket in the ship-armorer's rack. (123–24)

Imbued with the meaning and suggesting the shape of the whole book, and appearing at the climax of the narrative development, this moment fuses poetic concepts from earlier works and through their union gives birth to something new.

The poetic concepts that carry over involve both imagery and method. The association of Billy with the singing bird about to launch from the twig, confirming him as a symbol of harmony and as a captive in the world of war, has its forerunner in *White-Jacket* when, as the body of Shenly slides into the sea, Jack Chase calls a solitary bird overhead the spirit of the dead man-of-war's man, and all the crew gaze upward and watch it sail into the sky (lxxxi, 342). The use of sound and silence to convey the responses of the crew also has its precedent in *White-Jacket,* as has often been remarked, but here the direction is not from sound to silence but from silence to sound. The creation of a memorable, intensely visualizable scene to pictorialize the form and significance of a social institution is also a tested Melville method, most fully developed in *Benito Cereno.* Vividly signified in this scene are the war machine's concentration of power, its sacrifice of what is beautiful and good, and its "abrogation of everything but brute Force." It uncovers the ironies and contradictions of the situation: Vere in whom power is centered suffers the most; his humanity is seen to be totally repressed as he stands "erectly rigid as a musket in the ship armorer's rack." At the very moment the humanity in the crew is touched and they react in harmony with Billy, Vere becomes a thing of war whose sole function it is to mete out death, as Ahab at the end is no more than an extension of his weapon. Death-in-life in Vere stands in contrast with Life-in-death in Billy. The benediction, "God bless Captain Vere," gives voice to the feeling shared by Billy and Melville that Vere is the one on the *Bellipotent* most in need of blessing.

The way in which sight and sound are combined in this scene constitutes the new technique Melville's imagination brings forth in this crucial "penultimate moment" on the edge of both death and dawn. What is visual and what is aural join in a strange counterpoint wherein one element is held motionless while the other moves, each working simultaneously both with and against the other, to convey at one and the same moment the seemingly forever fixed picture of the present civilization of the world and movement stirring within it. It is as if in a film action were arrested and the sound continued. The tableau including Billy, the crew, and Vere impresses on the mind a picture that strikingly exhibits the established pattern of the world. It is the picture Vere wishes the admonitory spectacle to impress. But the aural accompaniment flows forward, carrying first Billy's benediction and then the sympathetic, swelling echo from the sailors in whose hearts he is. While what the mind's eye sees is frozen and motionless, the moving sound suggests that the frozen structure may thaw. Something in the heart of the crew, long asleep but intact, has been stirred. The tension between sight and sound, between the apparently immutable form and the growth of feeling within, will continue to the point at which the idea that a seed of change is germinating inside the rigid form will take the ascendancy, giving the work its positive tone. The unusual use of sight and sound in this climactic scene seems to grow out of Melville's desire, newly born in the course of the composition of *Billy Budd,* to explore how the seemingly eternal world of war might begin to be transformed to that fluid, life-giving world of peace so suddenly and startingly pictured—without any gradual transition to it—in the "Epilogue" to *Moby-Dick.*

As the signal for the hanging is given, a movement in the sky also creates a contrast with the formalized sight below. A cloud of vapor low in the East is "shot through with a soft glory as of the fleece of the Lamb of God seen in a mystical vision, and simultaneously therewith, watched by a wedged mass of upturned faces, Billy ascended; and, ascending, took the full rose of the dawn" (124), his spirit welcomed back into heaven.[16] The climax of the exemplary spectacle the crew has been forced to witness turns out to be one to inspire, one to move the heart and work as a dynamic in the imagination.

The short chapter culminating in the execution closes: "In the pinioned figure arrived at the yard-end, to the wonder of all no motion was apparent, none save that created by the slow roll of the hull in moderate weather, so majestic in a ship ponderously cannoned" (124). The sentence translates into visibility an earlier statement concerning the ordinary sailor: "Accustomed to obey

orders without debating them," he lives a life "externally ruled for
him" (87). Billy's "impotence," noted earlier by Vere when the
young sailor could not speak up against Claggart, is now realized
by the lack of any motion originating within his own body, which
is externally ruled by the "majestic" motion of His Majesty's Ship
Bellipotent. His impotence is in sharpest contrast with the omnipo-
tence of the captain who now stands erect as a musket, symbol of
civilization's ultimate Force. And yet the world of war, as *White-
Jacket* notes near the end, is "full of strange contradictions" (xci,
390). Billy does have power. Though impotent to save himself, he
has power to invoke the future. His death, illuminating the nature
of the world represented by the *Bellipotent,* will quicken the imagination of the crew and in that respect be a good death. But Vere,
the king's all-powerful representative, is, in a sense, the impotent
victim of the ultimate power concentrated in him. While Billy has
the miraculous ability to inspire love for a peaceful way of living,
to be in that sense a savior, Vere's potency is only for death. Like
Lot's wife, as Melville saw her in *White-Jacket,* he stands "crystal-
lized in the act of looking backward, and forever incapable of looking before" (xxxvi, 150). Hence Melville's execution scene is
symbolic of both the polarization of power in the world of war and
of the contradictions at the heart of such a world, contradictions
that must eventually bring a metamorphosis. They have already
caused a crack in the rigid mold; the silence, the aural equivalent
of the frozen form, has been broken. Eventually music (the ballad)
will issue through the fissure in the seemingly unbreakable form.

Moments after the execution the silence is "gradually disturbed
by a sound not easily to be verbally rendered." The sound is an
omen of a growth of feeling in the crew. "Whoever has heard *the
freshet-wave of a torrent suddenly swelled* by pouring showers in tropical
mountains, showers not shared by the plain; whoever has heard
the *first muffled murmur of its sloping advance through precipitous woods*
may form some conception of the sound now heard. The seeming
remoteness of its source was because of its murmurous indistinct-
ness, since it came from close by, even from the men massed on the
ship's open deck" (126, my emphasis). Only seemingly remote, the
source is deep within the men. The murmur is indistinct, but there
has been some expression, though wordless, of a feeling going back

to man's remote origin, and still latent within him. Then, like the "shriek of the sea hawk, the silver whistles of the boatswain and his mates pierced that ominous low sound, dissipating it" (126). The men, yielding to the mechanism of discipline, disperse, and the sound is, for the moment, silenced.

But, again, as the closing "formality" consigns Billy's body to the ocean, "a second strange human murmur" is heard from the sailors as vultures fly screaming to circle the spot (127). To the crew the action of the vultures, "though dictated by mere animal greed for prey," is "big with no prosaic significance," a phrase that earlier in the growth of the manuscript had read, "big with imaginative import of bale" (416). Though no elaboration follows, the unprosaic significance seems to involve human, as opposed to "mere animal," greed for prey and hints at an awakening of poetic sensibility to the meaning behind the sacrifice of Billy.

An uncertain movement begins among the men, to be counteracted by a drumbeat to quarters not customary at that hour. Vere intends the ensuing ritual to reimpose a strict pattern of conditioned response: " 'With mankind,' he would say, 'forms, measured forms, are everything; and that is the import couched in the story of Orpheus with his lyre spellbinding the wild denizens of the wood' " (128). The crew's unresisting participation in the formalities seems to bear out his theory; for "toned by music and religious rites subserving the discipline and purposes of war, the men in their wonted orderly manner dispersed to the places allotted them when not at the guns." But while the day which has followed the rosy dawn brings the firm reimposition of the military forms, "the circumambient air in the clearness of its serenity" is "like smooth white marble in the polished block not yet removed from the marble-dealer's yard" (128); the uncut marble of future time contains the possibility of being shaped into something different from the static form visible on the deck of the *Bellipotent.*

This introduction of the idea of a freer, more dynamic form is followed at once by a passage about form which bridges the now completed account of "How it fared with the Handsome Sailor during the year of the Great Mutiny" (128) and the three remaining chapters, "in way of sequel," which will embody Melville's creative concept of form and its meaning for him, the writer: "The symmetry of form attainable in pure fiction cannot so readily be achieved in a narration essentially having less to do with fable than with fact. Truth uncompromisingly told will always have its ragged edges; hence the conclusion of such a narration is apt to be less finished than an architectural finial" (128). The counterposition of the two statements about form, Vere's and Melville's, accents the fundamental difference between the thinking of the artist and the man of war. To Vere men are beasts to be tamed, "wild denizens of the wood," who must be bound. Brutishness is their sole potentiality. Melville, whose narrative has just revealed the humanity latent in men, evidenced by the crew's intuitive response to Billy, and has shown the men moved (unbound), has had Vere, the military man, speak of Orpheus, the artist, and find in his music only something akin to that "subserving the discipline and purposes of war." While to Vere war is a sacred, fated form and the *Bellipotent* a place of worship whose architecture is complete, to Melville that architecture is neither holy nor final. Vere would bind man's consciousness; Melville would awaken it. The conclusion of *Billy Budd* will be "less finished than an architectural finial" because Melville's art strives to be an equation of life, and life to him has no final form—a main theme in *Moby-Dick*. It may seem immutable, but within its set and apparently eternal form there are grains at work. Vere's ideas are to Melville's as long settled, measured, closed, and static form is to the fresh, open, living, growing shape into which the work is about to bloom. The realization of this new shape is a creative act by Melville closely related to his breaking out of the rigid circle of the chase at the end of *Moby-Dick*. The concluding chapters—a "sequel" in the sense of a necessary consequence—burst out of the established pattern of conventional narration and in so doing convey the idea that the rigid form of the world that has been pictured can also be disturbed.

The first of the chapters relates Vere's death. Last seen as a musket, he is himself struck by a musket ball. The incident (129) occurs on the return voyage to rejoin the fleet, when the *Bellipotent* encounters the French battleship, the *Athée* (the *Atheist*), "the aptest name, if one consider it, ever given to a warship." If it is the aptest name ever given a warship, it is the aptest name for the *Bellipotent,* and *bellipotence* and *atheism* become synonymous. Vere's death on the heels of his sacrifice of Billy to Mars is Melville's Judgment upon him for his denial of God. He does not permit Vere to be rewarded even in the way a votary of Mars must desire: "Unhappily he was cut off too early for the Nile and Trafalgar. The spirit that spite its philosophic austerity may yet have indulged in the most secret of all passions, ambition, never attained to the fulness of fame" (129). Like the dream of the admiral in "The Haglets," Vere's dreams of glory in war, if he had them (and one knows that early in the book excessive love of glory was described as the first "virtue" in a military man), are not realized.

But the account of his death reveals that even in Vere in whom man's humanity has been so determinedly suppressed, it is not dead: "Not long before death, while lying under the influence of that magical drug which, soothing the physical frame, *mysteriously operates on the subtler element in man,* he was heard to murmur words inexplicable to his attendant: 'Billy Budd, Billy Budd' " (129; my emphasis). The drug has freed the subconscious part of him from the silence he has imposed upon it, and his murmur unites with the "strange human murmur" of the crew. Surely, the passage implies, the silence of man's suppressed humanity will be breached if the heart of even this most austere monk of war speaks out. "Billy Budd, Billy Budd" is humankind's unconscious yearning for peace. It may be that the book's subtitle, *An Inside Narrative,* refers to what is occurring inside the heart of man in the critical modern era, continuing into Melville's day, which *Billy Budd* exemplifies.[17]

Vere's "Billy Budd, Billy Budd" is his exit line from the drama, and he will not be heard of again. Who "essentially" has he been? The contradictions carefully worked into his characterization—sometimes interpreted as evidence of carelessness or indecision on Melville's part—have been the source of opposite extremes of opinion among critics, all but a few of whom have been impressed by one side of him to the virtual exclusion of the other. But the contradiction within Vere is his very essence; the split in him is as central to his meaning as is the split in Ahab. He is the symbolic figure—not crudely, but finely and fairly, drawn—of civilized man: learned, but not sufficiently imaginative; not devoid of the ability to love, but not allowing this capacity to develop; sensitive to the difference between the good and evil signified by Billy and Clag-

gart, but the puppet of the god he has been trained to think must
rule in this world. His ultimate faith is in Force, not only against
the enemy, but in dealing with his own side—utilizing impressment, flogging, and hanging—and in dealing violently with his
own heart. Exceptional among the officers on the *Bellipotent,* and
even among captains, in his rigidity—there are over a score of references to, or images of, this quality always so appalling to Melville—
he is the comprehensive figure of what is dominant in modern
civilization. The contradiction within him is the contradiction
within it, between war's values and the primeval and enduring
needs of human beings. In Vere, as in civilization, there exist two
potentials—the one symbolized by the devil of war operating
through Claggart and the other signified by Billy as the peace-
loving angel of God—God and the devil continuing to be, as elsewhere in Melville's writing, poetic concepts signifying human
potentialities and values. It is the tragedy of civilized man, as of
Vere—tragic in the sense that creative potentialities are wasted—
that he has so far continued to uphold the values symbolized by
Claggart [18] and sacrifice those signified by Billy.

As if to underline the idea that the dream of glory in war is
doomed, Vere's name is not mentioned in the "authorized" naval
account of the *Bellipotent* events quoted in the chapter immediately
following his death.[19] The report is Melville's final illustration of
how good and evil are interchanged in the world of war and of
how "authorized" history may pervert the truth or use it for its
own purposes. The article reports Billy's "extreme depravity,"
while Claggart is said to have been "respectable and discreet," a
petty officer

> upon whom, as none know better than the commissioned gen-
> tlemen, the efficiency of His Majesty's navy so largely de-
> pends. His function was a responsible one, at once onerous
> and thankless; and his fidelity in it the greater because of his
> strong patriotic impulse. . . . The criminal paid the penalty of
> his crime. The promptitude of the punishment has proved
> salutary. Nothing amiss is now apprehended aboard H.M.S.
> *Bellipotent.* (130–31)

But Melville sees everything amiss—except for this, that whereas the report finds that the authorities have nothing "now" to apprehend (in the sense of fear), the crew has begun to apprehend (to be aware of) the fact that something must be amiss, as the concluding chapter (131-32) opens to view.

With no reason to worship Mars, though they are forced to take part in war's rites, with no illusion that war can satisfy for them "the most secret of all passions, ambition," the crew, inspired by Billy and groping toward some understanding of the mystery surrounding his hanging, has had engraved in its memory the execution scene that Melville has impressed upon the reader's. From ship to ship their "knowledges" follow the spar from which Billy was hanged. "To them a chip of it was as a piece of the Cross." And on the gundecks of the *Bellipotent* their "general estimate of his nature . . . eventually found rude utterance from another foretopman, one of his own watch, gifted, as some sailors are, with an artless *poetic* temperament. The tarry hand made some lines which, after circulating among the shipboard crews for a while, finally got rudely printed at Portsmouth as a ballad. The title given to it was the sailor's." So the inarticulate crew has found its voice. Feelings which had been only a murmur have "found utterance" not only in words but in poetry, however rude. The sailor-poet speaks for the men, unlike the song writer Dibdin described early in the book as "no mean auxiliary to the English government" (55). The sailor's lines are "finally" printed, as the feelings of the crew are "eventually" worded; a slow process is under way. And the ballad, "Billy in the Darbies" goes on to have a life of its own. In this way is Billy resurrected.

"Billy in the Darbies" (132), with which the book ends, is not the ballad as Melville originally conceived of it, the one that had given rise to the narration that was at first intended only to provide necessary background in an explanatory headnote. Early in the development of the work an organic interaction between the poem and the prose came into being, and as the narrative's implications grew, changes took place in the ballad as well and in its role in the book. An older Billy, who probably had plotted mutiny, gave way to a Billy not out of tune with the one in the story, and the ballad, originally intended as an expression of Billy's actual thoughts on the eve of his execution, became Billy's thoughts only as imagined at the end by the sailor-poet. As harmonies evolved between the poem and the prose, the poetry took on meanings implied by its words and images only in the context of the work as a whole. As it now stands, so integrated are the ballad and the rest of the book that the awakening feeling of the crew, as voiced by the sailor-poet, and Melville's own growing sense of the possibilities implicit in the internal contradictions of the world of war burst simultaneously into flower in the ballad.

In its last stage and final context "Billy in the Darbies" is extraordinarily subtle and complex. Yet Melville is utterly honest with the reader when he calls the gift of the sailor-poet an artless one. For it is Melville's art—as he speaks indirectly through the sailor's artlessness—which is sophisticated in the extreme. To read the ballad as the sailor's creation is prerequisite to appreciating it as Melville's.

The sailor identifies with Billy on the eve of his execution. He feels with him that the chaplain is good to pray for someone lowly like him. He sees the moonlight; he experiences Billy's fear, his hunger for companionship and food, the pressure of the handcuffs. He intends no symbolism, no irony, no complicated double meanings, only a few childlike puns. Yet, there is the beginning of questioning: "But aren't it all sham?" There is a dawning of consciousness of the grim sacrifice war exacts and men accede to: "But—no! It is dead then I'll be, *come to think*" (my emphasis). He sees a correspondence between Billy and another sailor whose cheek as he sank was also roseate, and feels the tie that unites them all. He has a growing feeling of being constricted; the oozy weeds twist about his body and hold him, too, down as he senses the reality that *White-Jacket* says "forever slides along far under the surface" of the sea on which the man of war sails ("The End," 399).

Melville's imagination works through the sailor's; his voice sounds in the overtones with which the narrative has endowed the sailor's simple words. The sailor's descriptive title is Melville's symbolic one: Billy Budd, sailor, lies in the darbies of war, from which he and all other sailors need to be released. He is a pearl of great beauty about to be jettisoned by the man-of-war world and "all adrift to go," like the drifted treasure in "The Haglets." For whom should the chaplain pray if not for "the likes" of him? One of the lowliest on the warship, Billy will, in a nonliteral way, go "aloft from alow": as he ascends the yard-end his goodness will convey an inspiration of true glory that at some future time may prove the salvation of all sailors on what White-Jacket in "The End" sees as "this earth that sails through the air."

Suggestive plays upon words, as Melville speaks through the language of the sailor, develop main themes of the prose. The "dawning of Billy's last day" will bring also the dawn of consciousness to the crew. "Heaven knows," indeed, who is responsible for the running of Billy up. The sailor's wondering query, "But aren't it all sham?" is Melville's implied question to the reader: "Isn't it all—the whole religion practiced in the *Bellipotent* 'cathedral'—a grotesque perversion of the religion whose music and rites it exploits but whose God in effect it denies?" A "blur" has been in man's eyes, his vision obscured by war and false songs and stories of war. He has been a child "dreaming."

The sailor-poet's linking of Billy with Bristol Molly, Donald (whoever he is), and Taff the Welshman signifies Melville's sense of the common humanity of man for which Billy has stood, the "one heart-beat at heart-core" felt by John Marr,[20] the "common sympathy" with his five hundred "fellow-beings" on the *Neversink* experienced by White-Jacket, his interest "ever after" in their welfare (xlii, 174), and the real communion and feeling of peace among men that Ishmael knows as he squeezes the whale's sperm with his "co-laborers" in the *Pequod*'s crew and forgets his "horrible oath" to wage Ahab's war (xciv, 348–49).

By making the ballad the work of a sailor-poet speaking for the crew whose dormant spirit of harmony Billy has awakened, Melville suggests a coming transfiguration of men and the world. While Billy's body lies bound by the weeds fathoms down, pictorializing the subterranean reality of war as White-Jacket pictures it (lxx, 294), as well as the good submerged in man but still capable of resurrection, his memory prompts in the imagination of the crew a subconscious quest for the meaning of his death, an inquiry that may someday ascend to full consciousness. In contrast to Vere who at the trial had spoken of the "mystery of iniquity" but had turned away from probing it, disclaiming moral responsibility, Melville is engaged in fathoming both the mystery of iniquity in the world and the mysterious potency of good. Since good can inspire mankind, even after the death of one epitomizing it, the ballad about Billy's physical end is not an architectural finial, either of the book or of the world it portrays.

The hanging of Billy has been translated into art (both by the sailor-poet and Melville), which in its interaction with life may give rise to a conscious desire by man to change his mode of existence. The *Bellipotent* form is not an inescapable part of the human condition but the result of the failure so far of man's heart and imagination to attempt to understand its mystery and to seek out the transforming possibility within it. Melville's imagination, as it makes itself known in all his works, even the most bitter, does not see civilization's forms as static, complete, devoid of all potentiality for "promoted life." [21] It is incapable of "that unfeeling acceptance of destiny which is promulgated in the name of service or tradition." [22]

So Melville in *Billy Budd* has shown the world of war, which "fallen" man created and then worshiped, in all its contradictions and potentiality, and his final emphasis has been on the creative in man and on the power of language and art to explore new values and inspire a fresh conception of life. He has written not of original sin but of original good and its continued, though sleeping existence in man, while evil—outstandingly exemplified in war—has been shown as a depravity in man, a fall from his inborn creative potentiality. As far back as the second chapter Melville had introduced this theme, but its deeper meaning for the work had not then been clear:

> it is observable that where certain virtues pristine and unadulterate peculiarly characterize anybody in the external uniform of civilization, they will upon scrutiny seem not to be derived from custom or convention, but . . . transmitted from a period prior to Cain's city and citified man. The character marked by such qualities has to an unvitiated taste an untampered-with flavor like that of berries, while the man thor-

oughly civilized, even in a fair specimen of the breed, has to the same moral palate a questionable smack as of a compounded wine. (52–53)

"Human nature" is not under attack here, but what civilization has done to deprave it is. What we have seen in Vere is that his human nature has been so tampered with that he believes he is "not authorized" to determine matters on the "primitive basis" of "essential right and wrong" (103) and that he must fight against his most natural emotions, his "primitive instincts strong as the wind and the sea" (109). On the other hand, primitive good, as symbolized by Billy, has been seen to be too childlike to be able to survive in the present civilization of the world. To transform the institutions of civilization so that good and beauty can thrive in an environment of peace, the members of the crew of man have to develop the desire to probe civilization's nature and articulate their needs and dreams. They must, in terms of the imagery relating to "Baby" Budd, attain manhood. *Billy Budd* implies that this may yet be.

Thus, in this narrative of man's silence transmuted into poetry Melville uses his art to try to break the spell holding human beings captive in the marble "form" of war, to break the tyranny of the "religion" of war over the minds and acts of potentially creative man. His illumination that a transformation of mankind and of the world is conceivable—may even already be germinating in man's imagination—is the source of the radiance that suffuses the work from Billy's "God bless Captain Vere" on. *Billy Budd* is Melville's most searching exploration of war, reaching back to the beginning of man and his fall into "Cain's city" and forward to a re-creation of the world by humanity reawakened.

Notes

1. Herman Melville, *Billy Budd, Sailor (An Inside Narrative)*, reading and genetic texts edited from the manuscript with introduction and notes by Harrison Hayford and Merton M. Sealts, Jr. (Chicago: Univ. of Chicago Press, 1962), hereafter to be abbreviated in the text to *Billy Budd*. All references to *Billy Budd* are to this edition.

2. *Omoo* (Evanston: Northwestern Univ. Press and The Newberry Library, 1968), Ch. xxix, p. 108n.

3. I am counting from a few years prior to the composition of *Typee* in 1844–45, on the theory that imaginative activity arising from Melville's aversion to war did not suddenly begin when he began to write. Redburn's reactions to the Nelson statuary and to the recruiting posters in Liverpool must have been those Melville remembered from his first voyage in 1839. The description of the warships in the harbor of Nukuheva in sharp contrast to the beauty of the island comes across as something stamped on Melville's mind by what he actually saw and reacted to when the *Acushnet* arrived in the Marquesas in 1842 at the time of the French takeover of the islands. And at least some of the poetic concepts in *White-Jacket* expressing antipathy to war and to the war machine surely developed out of Melville's earlier feeling and imagining on the warship *United States* in 1843–44, just before he became a writer.

4. See "The Haglets" for reference to "holier palms" in contrast to war's trophies, *Selected Poems of Herman Melville,* ed. Hennig Cohen (New York: Doubleday, 1964), p. 113.

5. See pp. 2 and 28 in the introductory material by Hayford and Sealts in *Billy Budd, Sailor* on the growth of the manuscript and the history of *Billy Budd* criticism.

6. Above all, I refer to these additions and amendments: modifications in the characters, their roles, and their interrelationships; the naming of the *Rights-of-Man* and the *Atheist* and the change of name from *Indomitable* to *Bellipotent;* introduction of Billy's vocal defect; augmentation of doubts regarding Vere's motivation, along with intensification of his suffering; introduction of the question of his sanity or insanity; addition of the chapter relating Vere's death and the time and manner of it; decisions about title, subtitle, and dedication; the resolution to end with the ballad and the change of the ballad from what Billy thought to what the sailor-poet imagines he thought on the eve of his execution; and the stated rejection of a settled, static "symmetry of form" leading into the "sequel."

7. *White-Jacket* (Evanston, Ill.: Northwestern Univ. Press and The Newberry Library, 1970), Ch. lxx, p. 293.

8. The abbreviation of this name to the *"Rights"* suggests that Melville had in mind not only those things to which men are entitled but also those things that are morally right, the rights that will be out of place in the environment to which Billy is to be transplanted. See Vere's discussion of their irrelevance (p. 110).

9. *Collected Poems of Herman Melville,* ed. Howard P. Vincent (Chicago: Hendricks House, 1947), p. 165.

10. *Selected Poems of Herman Melville,* ed. Robert Penn Warren (New York: Random House, 1970), p. 109.

11. *White-Jacket* had found both flogging and impressment to be against God. When a captain flogs a man, he is flogging the "image of his Creator" (Ch.

xxxiv, p. 142), and impressment is "an iniquity outrageous and insulting to God and man" (Ch. xc, p. 381n).

12. *Clarel* (New York: Hendricks House, 1960), Pt. IV, vii, p. 427.

13. *Moby-Dick* (New York: Norton, 1967) Ch. xxxiv, p. 131.

14. The fact that the passage is in the present tense strengthens the impression of this scene as a picture symbolic of what exists in the world, not just a picture of what Billy looked like at that particular past moment.

15. For a discussion of Elijah's role in the Old Testament and the New Testament as the eschatological forerunner of the coming Day of the Lord see entry, "Elijah the Prophet," in *The Interpreter's Dictionary of the Bible* (Nashville, Tenn.: Abingdon, 1962), II, pp. 88–90.

16. The correspondence Melville sets up between Billy and Christ (the "Lamb of God") is not a rigid one. Billy is associated also with the young Adam, Achilles, Apollo, and other non-Christian figures. Only those implications of the Christ story that harmonize with the other associations and implications of *Billy Budd* can logically be assumed to be Melville's.

17. Because of the validity of the comments of many who are concerned with women's liberation from the chains of language, I feel impelled to explain that I have used the words *man* and *mankind* rather than *humanity* as a rule in this chapter because they accord with Melville's imagery in *Billy Budd* and because I employ the word *humanity* for the most part in connection with what is human as distinguished from what is mechanical or merely animal in human beings' responses. Similarly, I have used the words *man* and *men* elsewhere in this book when they seemed to reflect Melville's way of thinking.

18. Despite their differences and the fact that Claggart is naturally distasteful to Vere, Melville subtly links them so that Claggart's warmaking can be seen as one side of present-day civilized man, the side to which he "veers": the word *austere* is repeatedly used in relation to both, and only to them, and civilization, "especially if of the austerer sort," which Vere represents, is "auspicious" to Claggartlike depravity; both are "discreet"; secrecy is a way both pursue; neither is sociable. Like Vere, Claggart is "zealous in his function" (p. 79). Claggart is "charged" (like a gun) with the duty of preserving order; Vere ends as "musket." Vere's final appeal to fear reminds the court of the dangers of mutiny, the very appeal Claggart had made to him in relation to Billy. Claggart's wish for Billy's death is ultimately carried out by Vere. Claggart acts against good; Vere rules out moral considerations. Both know Billy to be innocent, yet condemn him; as the devil operates through Claggart, so Mars operates through Vere.

19. Melville had at first made a pencil notation at this point in the book to speak, in the authorized report, of the death of Captain Vere, but he *canceled the notation* (pp. 269 and 420).

20. Vincent, p. 166.

21. Cohen, p. 53.

22. Wilson Harris, *Tradition, the Writer and Society* (London: New Beacon, 1967), p. 26.

Index

187